Chapter 4   Exchange

Chapter 5   Transport

Chapter 6   Genes and Cell division

Contents

Specification list

The specification labels on each page refer directly to the units in the exam specification, i.e. AQA ▶ 1.2 refers to unit 1, section 2.

AQA Biology

MODULE	SPECIFICATION TOPIC	CHAPTER REFERENCE	STUDIED IN CLASS	REVISED	PRACTICE QUESTIONS
Unit 1	Disease and lifestyle	8.1, 8.2			
	Digestion	3.3			
	Biological molecules	1.1,1.2,1.3,1.4			
	Enzymes	3.1, 3.2, 3.4			
	Cells and membrane transport	2.1, 2.2, 2.3, 4.1, 4.2, 8.2			
	The lungs and lung disease	4.3, 8.1			
	The heart and heart disease	5.2, 8.1			
	Immunity	8.3, 8.4			
Unit 2	Variation	7.2			
	DNA and the genetic code	6.1			
	Cell division	6.2			
	Biochemical differences	2.1, 1.2, 5.4			
	Cell differentiation	2.3			
	Transport	5.1, 5.3, 5.5			
	Gaseous exchange	4.4, 5.5			
	Classification	7.1			
	Mutation and variation	7.2			
	Biodiversity	7.2			

Examination analysis

Unit 1 – Examination paper (100 UMS) (60 raw marks) 5–7 short answer questions plus 2 longer questions, a short comprehension and a short structured essay 1¹/₄ hours 33.33% of the total AS marks 16.67% of the total A-level marks

Unit 2 – Examination paper (140 UMS) (85 raw marks) 7–9 short answer questions plus 2 longer questions (1 data handling and 1 assessing analysis and evaluation) 1³/₄ hours 46.67% of the total AS marks 23.33% of the total A-level marks

Unit 3 – Investigative and practical skills in AS Biology AS Centre Assessed Unit (60 UMS) (50 raw marks) Practical Skills Assessment (PSA) 6 marks, Investigative Skills Assignment (ISA) 44 marks, 20% of the total AS marks 10% of the total A-level marks

AS and A2

The AQA Biology A Level course being studied from September 2008 is in two parts, with a number of separate modules or units in each part. Most students will start by studying the AS (Advanced Subsidiary) course. Some will go on to study the second part of the A Level course, called A2. Advanced Subsidiary is assessed at the standard expected halfway through an A Level course, i.e. between GCSE and A Level. This means that the new AS and A2 courses are designed so that difficulty steadily increases:

- AS Biology builds from GCSE Science and Additional Science/Biology.
- A2 Biology builds from AS Biology.

How will you be tested?

Assessment units

AS Biology comprises three units or modules. The first two units are assessed by examinations. The third component involves practical assessment.

Centre-based practical assessment involves practical skills marked by your teacher. The marks can be adjusted by moderators appointed by the awarding body.

For AS Biology, you will be tested by three assessment units. For the full A Level in Biology, you will take a further three units. AS Biology forms 50% of the assessment weighting for the full A Level.

Tests are taken at two specific times of the year, January and June. It can be an advantage to you to take a unit test at the earlier optional time because you can re-sit the test. The best mark for each unit will be credited and the lower mark ignored.

Each unit can normally be taken in either January or June. Alternatively, you can study the whole course before taking any of the unit tests. There is a lot of flexibility about when exams can be taken and the following diagram shows just some of the ways that the assessment units may be taken for AS and A Level Biology.

Revise AS

AQA Biology

John Parker & Ian Honeysett

Contents

Chapter 1 Biological molecules

Chapter 2 Cells

Chapter 3 Enzymes

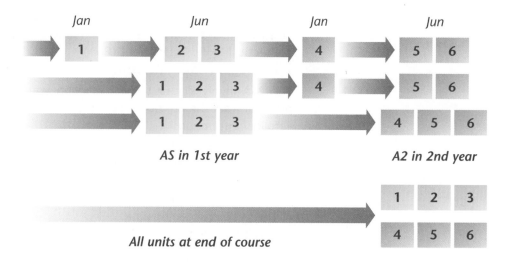

Jan *Jun* *Jan* *Jun*

AS in 1st year *A2 in 2nd year*

All units at end of course

A2 and synoptic assessment

Many students who have studied at AS Level may decide to go on to study A2. There are three further units or modules to be studied. The A Level specification includes a 'synoptic' assessment at the end of A2. Synoptic questions make use of concepts from earlier units, bringing them together in holistic contexts. Examiners will test your ability to inter-relate topics through the complete course from AS to A2.

Internal Assessment of Practical Skills

Internal assessment will form part of your A Level Biology course. It will be in the form of assessment of practical skills.

What skills will I need?

For AS Biology, you will be tested by assessment objectives: these are the skills and abilities that you should have acquired by studying the course. The assessment objectives for AS Biology are shown below.

Knowledge with understanding

- recall of facts, terminology and relationships
- understanding of principles and concepts
- drawing on existing knowledge to show understanding of the responsible use of biological applications in society
- selecting, organising and presenting information clearly and logically

Application of knowledge and understanding, analysis and evaluation

- explaining and interpreting principles and concepts
- interpreting and translating, from one to another, data presented as continuous prose or in tables, diagrams and graphs
- carrying out relevant calculations
- applying knowledge and understanding to familiar and unfamiliar situations
- assessing the validity of biological information, experiments, inferences and statements

You must also present arguments and ideas clearly and logically, using specialist vocabulary where appropriate. Remember to balance your argument!

Investigative and practical skills

One of the three AS units (and one of the A2 units) is designed to test your investigative and practical skills. Each unit is made up of two parts:

- **Practical Skills Assessment (PSA)**
- **Investigative Skills Assessment (ISA)**

The **PSA** involves your teacher marking you on a scale 0 to 6 based on your practical work throughout the course. They will be looking to see if you can...

- follow instructions
- select and use equipment
- carry out practical work in an organised and safe way.

The **ISA** carries 44 marks and is made up of three tasks:

- First you collect some practical data
- Then you process the data
- This is followed by a written paper relating to the experiment.

These ISA tasks are provided by AQA and you will carry them out under controlled conditions, being supervised by your teacher. Your teacher then marks them using a mark scheme provided by AQA. A task cannot be repeated but you may be given the opportunity to do more than one of each type of task. Your best mark on each will count. (There is an alternative to the ISA which is provided and marked by AQA. Only one of these is provided each year.)

It is important in these tasks to know the difference between **validity**, **reliability**, **precision** and **accuracy**.

- **Validity:** in a valid experiment you only investigate one variable at a time. All the other variables are kept constant. This means that you are really measuring what you are trying to measure.
- **Reliability:** an experiment is reliable if it can be repeated and similar results are obtained. Reliability is usually be increased by taking repeat readings and averaging them.
- **Accuracy:** an accurate measurement is one that is close to an accepted value. This accepted value is usually the work of many scientists and can be checked from accepted sources.
- **Precision:** If an experiment is precise it means that readings can be made to a number of significant digits and that similar results can be made each time.

The best way to describe the difference between accuracy and precision is to use the example of a darts board:

These darts are precise because they are all close to each other, but they are not very accurate.

These darts are precise because they are all close to each other and are accurate.

These darts are not very precise, nor very accurate.

Different types of questions in AS examinations

In AS Biology examinations different types of questions are used to assess your abilities and skills. Unit tests mainly use structured questions requiring both short-answers and more extended answers.

Short-answer questions

A question will normally begin with a brief amount of stimulus material. This may be in the form of a diagram, data or graph. A short-answer question may begin by testing recall. Usually this is followed up by questions which test understanding. Often you will be required to analyse data.

Short-answer questions normally have a space for your responses on the printed paper. The number of lines is a guide as to the amount of words you will need to answer the question. The number of marks indicated on the right side of the paper shows the number of marks you can score for each question part.

Here are some examples. (The answers are shown in blue)

The diagram shows part of a DNA molecule.

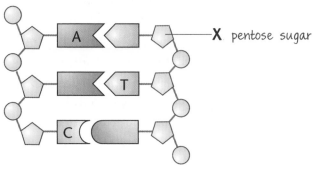

(a) Label part X. [1]

(b) Complete the diagram by writing a letter for each missing organic base in each empty box. [1]

(b) How do two strands of DNA join to each other?

The organic bases ✓ link the strands by hydrogen bonds ✓ [2]

Structured questions

Structured questions are in several parts. The parts are usually about a common context and they often progress in difficulty as you work through each of the parts. They may start with simple recall, then test understanding of a familiar or unfamiliar situation. If the context seems unfamiliar the material will still be centred around concepts and skills from the Biology specification. (If a student can answer questions about unfamiliar situations then they display understanding rather than simple recall.)

The most difficult part of a structured question is usually at the end. Ascending in difficulty, a question allows a candidate to build in confidence. Right at the end technological and social applications of biological principles give a more demanding challenge. Most of the questions in this book are structured questions. This is the main type of question used in the assessment of AS Biology.

When answering structured questions, do not feel that you have to complete a question before starting the next. Answering a part that you are sure of will build your confidence. If you run out of ideas go on to the next question. This will be more profitable than staying with a very difficult question which slows down progress. Return at the end when you have more time.

Here is an example of a structured question which becomes progressively more demanding.

Question

The diagram shows the molecules of a cell surface membrane.

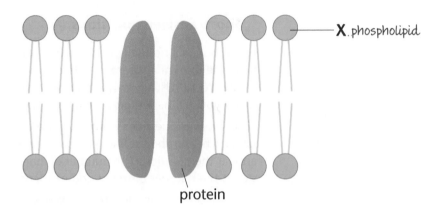

(a) (i) Label molecule X.   [1]

(ii) The part of molecule X facing the outside of a cell is hydrophilic. What does this mean?

water loving/water attracting   [1]

(iii) Describe **one** feature of the part of molecule X which faces inwards.

Hydrophobic/ water hating fatty acid residues   [1]

(b) Explain how the protein shown in the diagram can actively transport the glucose molecule into the cell.

Energy is released from mitochondria near the channel protein the channel protein opens   [3]

Note the help given in diagrams. The labelling of the protein molecule may trigger the memory so that the candidate has to make a small step to link the 'channel' function to this diagram. Examiners give clues! Expect more clues at AS Level than at A2 Level.

Extended answers

In AS Biology, questions requiring more extended answers will usually form part of structured questions. They will normally appear at the end of a structured question and will typically have a value of three to six marks. Longer answers are allocated more lines, so you can use this as a guide as to the extent of your answer. The mark allocation is a guide as to how many points you need to make in your response. Often for an answer worth six marks the mark scheme could have eight creditable answers. You are awarded up to the maximum, six in this instance.

Depending on the awarding body, longer extended questions may be set. These are often open response questions. These questions may be worth up to ten marks for full credit. Extended answers are used to allocate marks for the quality of written communication.

Candidates are assessed on their ability to use a suitable style of writing, and organise relevant material, both logically and clearly. The use of specialist biological words in context is also assessed. Spelling, punctuation and grammar are also taken into consideration. Here is a longer extended response question.

Question

Give an account of the effects of sewage entry into a river and explain the possible consequences to organisms downstream.

The sewage enters the river and is decomposed by bacteria. ✓ These bacteria are saprobiotic ✓ they produce nitrates which act as a fertiliser. ✓ Algae form a blanket on the surface ✓ light cannot reach plants under the algae so these plants die. ✓ Bacteria decompose the dead plants ✓ the bacteria use oxygen/bacteria are aerobic ✓ fish die due to lack of oxygen ✓ Tubifex worms or bloodworms increase near sewage entry ✓ mayfly larvae cannot live close to sewage entry/mayfly larvae appear a distance downstream where oxygen levels return. ✓

10 marking points → [7]

Remember that mark schemes for extended questions often exceed the question total, but you can only be awarded credit up to a maximum. Examiners sometimes build in a hurdle, e.g. in the above responses, references to one organism which increases in population is worthy of a mark, and another which decreases in population is worth another. Continually referring to different species which repeat a growth pattern will not gain further credit.

Exam technique

Links from GCSE

AS Biology builds from grade C in GCSE Science and GCSE Additional Science (combined) or GCSE Biology. This study guide has been written so that you will be able to tackle AS Biology from a GCSE science background.

You should not need to search for important Biology from GCSE science because this has been included where needed in each chapter. If you have not studied science for some time, you should still be able to learn AS Biology using this text alone.

What are examiners looking for?

Whatever type of question you are answering, it is important to respond in a suitable way. Examiners use instructions to help you to decide the length and depth of your answer. The most common words used are given below, together with a brief description of what each word is asking for.

Define

This requires a formal statement. Some definitions are easy to recall.

Define the term active transport.

This is the movement of molecules from where they are in lower concentration to where they are in higher concentration. The process requires energy.

Other definitions are more complex. Where you have problems it is helpful to give an example.

Define the term endemic.

This means that a disease is found regularly in a group of people, district or country. Use of an example clarifies the meaning. Indicating that malaria is invariably found everywhere in a country, confirms understanding.

Explain

This requires a reason. The amount of detail needed is shown by the number of marks allocated.

Explain the difference between resolution and magnification.

Resolution is the ability to be able to distinguish between two points whereas magnification is the number of times an image is bigger than an object itself.

State

This requires a brief answer without any reason.

State one role of blood plasma in a mammal.

Transport of hormones to their target organs.

List

This requires a sequence of points with no explanation.

List the abiotic factors which can affect the rate of photosynthesis in pond weed.

carbon dioxide concentration; amount of light; temperature; pH of water

Describe

This requires a piece of prose which gives key points. Diagrams should be used where possible.

Describe the nervous control of heart rate.

The medulla oblongata ✓ of the brain connects to the sino atrial node in the right atrium, wall ✓ via the vagus nerve and the sympathetic nerve ✓ the sympathetic nerve speeds up the rate ✓ the vagus nerve slows it down. ✓

Discuss

This requires points both for and against, together with a criticism of each point. (**Compare** is a similar command word.)

Discuss the advantages and disadvantages of using systemic insecticides in agriculture.

Advantages are that the insecticides kill the pests which reduce yield ✓ they enter the sap of the plants so insects which consume sap die ✓ the insecticide lasts longer than a contact insecticide, 2 weeks is not uncommon ✓

Disadvantages are that insecticide may remain in the product and harm a consumer e.g. humans ✓ it may destroy organisms other than the target ✓ no insecticide is 100% effective and develops resistant pests. ✓

Suggest

This means that there is no single correct answer. Often you are given an unfamiliar situation to analyse. The examiners hope for logical deductions from the data given and that, usually, you apply your knowledge of biological concepts and principles.

The graph shows that the population of lynx decreased in 1980. Suggest reasons for this.

Weather conditions prevented plant growth ✓ so the snowshoe hares could not get enough food and their population remained low ✓ so the lynx did not have enough hares(prey) to predate upon. ✓ The lynx could have had a disease which reduced numbers. ✓

Calculate

This requires that you work out a numerical answer. Remember to give the units and to show your working, marks are usually available for a partially correct answer. If you work everything out in stages write down the sequence. Otherwise if you merely give the answer and it is wrong, then the working marks are not available to you.

Calculate the Rf value of spot X. (X is 25 mm from start and solvent front is 100 mm)

$$Rf = \frac{\text{distance moved by spot}}{\text{distance moved by the solvent front}}$$

$$= \frac{25 \text{ mm}}{100 \text{ mm}}$$

$$= 0.25$$

Outline

This requires that you give only the main points. The marks allocated will guide you on the number of points which you need to make.

Outline the use of restriction endonuclease in genetic engineering.

The enzyme is used to cut the DNA of the donor cell. ✓

It cuts the DNA up like this A T G C C G A T = A T   + G C C G A T ✓
           T A C G G C T A   T A C G G C   T A

The DNA in a bacterial plasmid is cut with the same restriction endonuclease. ✓

The donor DNA will fit onto the sticky ends of the broken plasmid. ✓

If a question does not seem to make sense, you may have mis-read it. Read it again!

Some dos and don'ts

Dos

Do answer the question

No credit can be given for good Biology that is irrelevant to the question.

Do use the mark allocation to guide how much you write

Two marks are awarded for two valid points – writing more will rarely gain more credit and could mean wasted time or even contradicting earlier valid points.

Do use diagrams, equations and tables in your responses

Even in 'essay style' questions, these offer an excellent way of communicating biology.

Do write legibly

An examiner cannot give marks if the answer cannot be read.

Do write using correct spelling and grammar. Structure longer essays carefully

Marks are now awarded for the quality of your language in exams.

Don'ts

Don't fill up any blank space on a paper

In structured questions, the number of dotted lines should guide the length of your answer.

If you write too much, you waste time and may not finish the exam paper. You also risk contradicting yourself.

Don't write out the question again

This wastes time. The marks are for the answer!

Don't contradict yourself

The examiner cannot be expected to choose which answer is intended. You could lose a hard-earned mark.

Don't spend too much time on a part that you find difficult

You may not have enough time to complete the exam. You can always return to a difficult calculation if you have time at the end of the exam.

What grade do you want?

Everyone would like to improve their grades but you will only manage this with a lot of hard work and determination. You should have a fair idea of your natural ability and likely grade in biology and the hints below offer advice on improving that grade.

For a Grade A

You will need to be a very good all-rounder.

- You must go into every exam knowing the work extremely well.
- You must be able to apply your knowledge to new, unfamiliar situations.
- You need to have practised many, many exam questions so that you are ready for the type of question that will appear.

The exams test all areas of the syllabus and any weaknesses in your biology will be found out. There must be no holes in your knowledge and understanding. For a Grade A, you must be competent in all areas.

For a Grade C

You must have a reasonable grasp of biology but you may have weaknesses in several areas and you will be unsure of some of the reasons for the biology.

- Many Grade C candidates are just as good at answering questions as the Grade A students but holes and weaknesses often show up in just some topics.
- To improve, you will need to master your weaknesses and you must prepare thoroughly for the exam. You must become a better all-rounder.

For a Grade E

You cannot afford to miss the easy marks. Even if you find biology difficult to understand and would be happy with a Grade E, there are plenty of questions in which you can gain marks.

- You must memorise all definitions.
- You must practise exam questions to give yourself confidence that you do know some biology. In exams, answer the parts of questions that you know first. You must not waste time on the difficult parts. You can always go back to these later.
- The areas of biology that you find most difficult are going to be hard to score on in exams. Even in the difficult questions, there are still marks to be gained. Show your working in calculations because credit is given for a sound method. You can always gain some marks if you get part of the way towards the solution.

What marks do you need?

The table below shows how your average mark is transferred into a grade.

average	80%	70%	60%	50%	40%
grade	A	B	C	D	E

To achieve an A* grade, you need to achieve a...

- grade A overall (80% or more on uniform mark scale) for the **whole** A level qualification
- grade A* (90% or more on the uniform mark scale) across your A2 units.

A* grades are awarded for the A level qualification only and not for the AS qualification or individual units.

Four steps to successful revision

Step 1: Understand

- Study the topic to be learned slowly. Make sure you understand the logic or important concepts.
- Mark up the text if necessary – underline, highlight and make notes.
- Re-read each paragraph slowly.

GO TO STEP 2

Step 2: Summarise

- Now make your own revision note summary:
  What is the main idea, theme or concept to be learnt?
  What are the main points? How does the logic develop?
  Ask questions: Why? How? What next?
- Use bullet points, mind maps, patterned notes.
- Link ideas with mnemonics, mind maps, crazy stories.
- Note the title and date of the revision notes
  (e.g. Biology: Cells, 3rd March).
- Organise your notes carefully and keep them in a file.

This is now in **short-term memory**. You will forget 80% of it if you do not go to Step 3.
GO TO STEP 3, but first take a 10 minute break.

Step 3: Memorise

- Take 25 minute learning 'bites' with 5 minute breaks.
- After each 5 minute break test yourself:
  Cover the original revision note summary.
  Write down the main points.
  Speak out loud (record on tape).
  Tell someone else.
  Repeat many times.

The material is well on its way to **long-term memory**.
You will forget 40% if you do not do step 4. GO TO STEP 4

Step 4: Track/Review

- Create a Revision Diary (one A4 page per day).
- Make a revision plan for the topic, e.g. 1 day later, 1 week later, 1 month later.
- Record your revision in your Revision Diary, e.g.
  Biology: Cells, 3rd March 25 minutes
  Biology: Cells, 5th March 15 minutes
  Biology: Cells, 3rd April 15 minutes
  ... and then at monthly intervals.

Biological molecules

The following topics are covered in this chapter:

- *Carbohydrates*
- *Lipids*
- *Proteins*

1.1 Carbohydrates

After studying this section you should be able to:

LEARNING SUMMARY

- *recall the main elements found in carbohydrates*
- *recall the structure of glucose, fructose, lactose, sucrose, starch, glycogen and cellulose*
- *recall the role of glucose, starch, glycogen, cellulose and pectin*

Structure of carbohydrates

AQA ▶ 1.2, 2.4

Monosaccharides

All carbohydrates are formed from the elements carbon (C), hydrogen (H) and oxygen (O). The formula of a carbohydrate is always $(CH_2O)_n$. The n represents the number of times the basic CH_2O unit is repeated, e.g. where n = 6 the molecular formula is $C_6H_{12}O_6$. This is the formula shared by glucose and other simple sugars like fructose. These simple sugars are made up from a single sugar unit and are known as monosaccharides.

The molecular formula, $C_6H_{12}O_6$, does not indicate how the atoms bond together. Bonded to the carbon atoms are a number of – H and – OH groups. Different positions of these groups on the carbon chain are responsible for different properties of the molecules. The structural formulae of α and β glucose are shown below.

> These molecules are mirror images of each other. When molecules have the same molecular formula but different structural formulae, they are known as **isomers**. Isomers have different properties to each other.

α glucose   β glucose

Glucose is so small that it can pass through the villi and capillaries into our bloodstream. The molecules subsequently release energy as a result of respiration. Simple glucose molecules are capable of so much more than just releasing energy. They can combine with others to form bigger molecules.

Disaccharides

Each glucose unit is known as a monomer and is capable of linking others. This diagram shows two molecules of α glucose forming a disaccharide.

> In your examinations look for different monosaccharides being given, like fructose or β glucose. You may be asked to show how they bond together. The principle will be exactly the same.

α glucose   α glucose

H_2O condensation reaction

maltose

A condensation reaction means that as two carbohydrate molecules bond together a water molecule is produced. The link formed between the two glucose molecules is known as a glycosidic bond.

A glycosidic bond can also be broken down to release separate monomer units. This is the opposite of the reaction shown above. Instead of water being given off, a water molecule is needed to break each glycosidic bond. This is called hydrolysis because water is needed to split up the bigger molecule.

> 'Lysis' literally means 'splitting'. In hydrolysis water is needed in the reaction to break down the molecule.

Different disaccharides are made by joining together different monosaccharides.

Disaccharide	Component monosaccharides
lactose	glucose + galactose
maltose	glucose + glucose
sucrose	glucose + fructose

Polysaccharides

Like disaccharides, polysaccharides consist of monomer units linked by the glycosidic bond. However, instead of just two monomer units they can have many. Chains of these 'sugar' units are known as polymers. These larger molecules have important structural and storage roles.

Starch is a polymer of the sugar, α glucose. The diagram below shows part of a starch molecule.

> Notice the five glycosidic bonds on just a small part of a starch molecule.

part of a branched section of a starch molecule

This type of starch molecule is called amylopectin and it has a branched structure. Starch also contains amylose. This does not contain branches but the chain of glucose units forms a helix. Glycogen is similar in structure to amylopectin but with more branches. Cellulose is also a polymer of glucose units, but this time the units are β glucose.

How useful are polysaccharides?

- Starch is stored in organisms as a future energy source, e.g. potato has a high starch content to supply energy for the buds to grow at a later stage.
- Glycogen is stored in the liver, which releases glucose for energy in times of low blood sugar.

Both starch and glycogen are insoluble which enables them to remain inside cells.

The many branches in the amylopectin molecule means that enzymes can digest the molecule rapidly.

- **Cellulose** has long molecules which help form a tough protective layer around plant cells, the cell wall. Each cellulose molecule has up to 10 000 β glucose units. Each molecule can form cross-links with other cellulose molecules forming fibres. This makes cellulose fibres very strong.

- **Pectins** are used alongside cellulose in the cell wall. They are polysaccharides which are bound together by calcium pectate.

Together the cellulose and pectins give exceptional mechanical strength. The cell wall is also permeable to a wide range of substances.

1.2 Lipids

What are lipids?

AQA 1.3

Lipids include **oils**, **fats** and **waxes**. They consist of exactly the same elements as carbohydrates, i.e. carbon (C), hydrogen (H) and oxygen (O), but their proportion is different. There is always a high proportion of carbon and hydrogen, with a small proportion of oxygen.

The diagram below shows the structural formula of the most common type of lipid called a **triglyceride**.

a **triglyceride** fat

Triglycerides are formed when fatty acids react with glycerol. During this reaction water is produced, a further example of a condensation reaction. The essential bond is the **ester bond**.

3 fatty acids   glycerol   a triglyceride fat   water

Triglycerides can be changed back into the original fatty acids and glycerol. Enzymes are needed for this transformation together with water molecules. Remember, an enzyme reaction which requires water to break up a molecule is known as **hydrolysis**.

The hydrocarbon chains are so long that they are often represented by the acid group (–COOH) and a zig-zag line.

unsaturated
∿∿∿=∿∿∿COOH

saturated
∿∿∿∿∿∿COOH

What are saturated and unsaturated fats?

The answer lies in the types of fatty acid used to produce them.

stearic acid

a **saturated** fatty acid

Saturated fats lead to cholesterol build up in the blood vessels so many people try to avoid them in their diet. Blocked vessels cause heart attacks.

oleic acid

an **unsaturated** fatty acid

Note that when saturated fatty acids react with glycerol they make saturated fats. Conversely, unsaturated fatty acids make unsaturated fats.

> **KEY POINT**
> Saturated fatty acids have no C=C (double bonds) in their hydrocarbon chain, but unsaturated fatty acids do. This is the difference.

How useful are lipids?

Like carbohydrates, lipids are used as an energy supply, but a given amount of lipid releases more energy than the same amount of carbohydrate. Due to their insolubility in water and compact structure, lipids have long-term storage qualities. Adipose cells beneath our skin contain large quantities of fat which insulate us and help to maintain body temperature. Fat gives mechanical support around our soft organs and even gives electrical insulation around our nerve axons.

An aquatic organism such as a dolphin has a large fat layer which:

* is an energy store
* is a thermal insulator
* helps the animal remain buoyant.

Never give an ambiguous answer like this: 'fats keep an animal warm'. The examiner does not know whether you are referring to energy release by mitochondria or the insulation property. Be specific, otherwise you will not be credited.

The most important role of lipids is their function in cell membranes. To fulfil these functions a triglyceride fat is first converted into a phospholipid.

triglyceride   phosphoric acid   phospholipid

Phosphoric acid replaces one of the fatty acids of the triglyceride. The new molecule, the phospholipid, is a major component of cell membranes. Cell membranes also contain the lipid cholesterol. The following diagram represents a phospholipid.

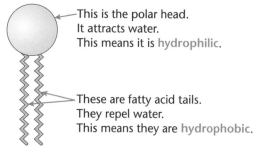

—This is the polar head.
It attracts water.
This means it is hydrophilic.

Remember this simplified diagram when you learn about the cell membrane.

—These are fatty acid tails.
They repel water.
This means they are hydrophobic.

a phospholipid

1.3 Proteins

The building blocks of proteins

AQA   1.2

Like carbohydrates and lipids, proteins contain the elements carbon (C), hydrogen (H) and oxygen (O), but in addition they **always** contain **nitrogen** (N). Sulfur is also often present.

Before understanding how proteins are constructed, the structure of **amino acids** should be noted. The diagram below shows the general structure of an amino acid.

Just like the earlier carbohydrate and lipid molecules, 'R' represents groups such as $-CH_3$ and $-C_2H_5$. There are about 20 commonly found amino acids but you will not need to know them all. Instead, learn the basic structure shown opposite.

amine group →

carboxylic acid group

an amino acid

How is a protein constructed?

The process begins by amino acids bonding together. The diagram shows two amino acids being joined together by a **peptide bond**.

This is another example of a condensation reaction as water is produced as the dipeptide molecule is assembled.

Note that the peptide bonds can be broken down by a hydrolysis reaction.

peptide bond

amino acid   amino acid   a dipeptide   + H_2O

When many amino acids join together a long-chain **polypeptide** is produced. The linking of amino acids in this way takes place during protein synthesis (see page 74). There are around 20 different amino acids. Organisms join amino acids in different linear sequences to form a variety of polypeptides, then build these polypeptides into complex molecules, the **proteins**. Humans need eight essential amino acids as adults and ten as children, all the others can be made inside the cells.

The sequence of amino acids along a polypeptide is controlled by another complex molecule, DNA (see the genetic code, page 73).

Levels of organisation in proteins

AQA ▷ 1.2

Primary protein structure

This is the linear sequence of amino acids.

Secondary protein structure

Polypeptides become twisted or coiled. These shapes are known as the secondary structure. There are two common secondary structures; the α-helix and the β-pleated sheet.

> Both secondary structures give additional strength to proteins. The α-helix helps make tough fibres like the protein in your nails, e.g. keratin. The β-pleated sheet helps make the strength-giving protein in silk, fibroin. Many proteins are made from both α-helix and β-pleated sheet.

The polypeptides are held in position by hydrogen bonds. In both α-helices and β-pleated sheets the $C = O$ of one amino acid bonds to the $H–N$ of an adjacent amino acid like this: $C = O \cdots H–N$.

----- = hydrogen bonds

An α-helix is a tight, twisted strand; a β-pleated sheet is where a zig-zag line of amino acids bonds with the next, and so on. This forms a sheet or ribbon shape.

> The protein shown only achieves a secondary structure as the simple α-helix polypeptides do not undergo further folding.
>
> This is the structure of a fibrous protein. It is made of three α-helix polypeptides twisted together.

coiled α-helix structure   a fibrous protein

Tertiary protein structure

> Note that the specific contours of proteins have extremely significant roles in life processes. (See enzymes page 40.)

This is when a polypeptide is folded into a precise shape. The polypeptide is held in 'bends' and 'tucks' in a permanent shape by a range of bonds including:

- disulfide bridges (sulfur–sulfur bonds)
- hydrogen bonds
- ionic bonds
- hydrophobic and hydrophilic interactions.

Some proteins are folded up into a spherical shape. They are called globular proteins. They are soluble in water. Other proteins, called fibrous proteins, form long chains. They are insoluble and usually perform structural functions.

This is the structure of a **globular** protein. It is made of an α-helix and a β-pleated sheet. Precise shapes are formed with specific contours.

Note that some proteins do not have a quaternary structure. If they consist of just one folded polypeptide then they are classified as having tertiary structure. If they are simple fibres of α-helices or β-pleated sheets then they have only secondary protein structure.

Quaternary protein structure

Some proteins consist of different polypeptides bonded together to form extremely intricate shapes. A haemoglobin molecule is formed from four separate polypeptide chains. It also has a haem group, which contains iron. This inorganic group is known as a prosthetic group and in this instance aids oxygen transport.

α-helix —— β-pleated sheet
—— disulfide bridge

a quaternary structure

How useful are proteins?

AQA ▸ 1.2

Proteins can be just as beneficial as carbohydrates and lipids in releasing energy. Broken down into their component amino acids, they liberate energy during respiration. The list below shows important uses of proteins:

- **cell-membrane proteins** transport substances across the membrane for processes such as facilitated diffusion and active transport
- **enzymes** catalyse biochemical reactions, e.g. pepsin breaks down protein into polypeptides
- **hormones** are passed through the blood and trigger reactions in other parts of the body, e.g. insulin regulates blood sugar
- **immuno-proteins**, e.g. antibodies are made by lymphocytes and act against antigenic sites on micro-organisms
- **structural proteins** give strength to organs, e.g. collagen makes tendons tough
- **transport proteins**, e.g. haemoglobin transports oxygen in the blood
- **contractile proteins**, e.g. actin and myosin help muscles shorten during contraction
- **storage proteins**, e.g. aleurone in seeds helps germination, and casein in milk helps supply valuable protein to babies
- **buffer proteins**, e.g. blood proteins, due to their charge, help maintain the pH of plasma.

Progress check

1 List the sequence of structures in a globular protein such as haemoglobin.

2 The following statements refer to proteins used for different functions in the body. The list gives the name of different types of protein. Match the name of each type of protein with the correct statement.

(i) transport proteins   (vi) contractile proteins
(ii) immuno-proteins   (vii) enzymes
(iii) storage proteins   (viii) structural proteins
(iv) buffer proteins   (ix) hormones
(v) cell-membrane proteins

A haemoglobin is used to transport oxygen in blood.

B aleurone in seeds is a source of amino acids as it is broken down during germination.

C actin and myosin help muscles shorten during contraction.

Progress check

D antibodies made by lymphocytes against antigens.

E blood proteins, due to their charge, help maintain the pH of plasma.

F used to transport substances across the membrane for processes such as facilitated diffusion.

G passed through blood, used to trigger reactions in other parts of the body, e.g. FSH stimulates a primary follicle.

H used to catalyse biochemical reactions, e.g. amylase breaks down starch into maltose.

I used to give strength to organs, e.g. collagen makes tendons tough.

2 A (i), B (iii), C (vi), D (ii), E (iv), F (v), G (ix), H (vii), I (viii).

1 primary structure: amino acids linked in a linear sequence; secondary structure: α-helix or β-pleated sheet; tertiary structure: further folding of polypeptide held by disulfide bridges, ionic bonds, and hydrogen bonds; quaternary structure: two or more polypeptides bonded together.

1.4 Biochemical tests

After studying this section you should be able to:

• describe biochemical tests for carbohydrates, lipids and proteins

LEARNING SUMMARY

Biochemical tests

AQA 1.2

All the biochemical tests need to be learned. This work is good value because they are regularly tested in 2 or 3 mark question components.

Tests for carbohydrates in the laboratory

Benedict's test used to identify reducing sugars (monosaccharides and some disaccharides)
• Add Benedict's solution to the chemical sample and heat.
• The solution changes from blue to brick-red or yellow if a reducing sugar is present.

Non-reducing sugar test used to test for non-reducing sugars, e.g. the disaccharide, sucrose
• First a Benedict's test is performed.
• If the Benedict's test is negative, the sample is hydrolysed by heating with hydrochloric acid, then neutralised with sodium hydrogen carbonate.
• This breaks the glycosidic bond of the disaccharide, releasing the monomers.
• A second Benedict's test is performed which will be positive because the monomers are now free.

Starch test
• Add iodine solution to the sample.
• If starch is present the colour changes to blue-black.

Tests for lipids in the laboratory

Emulsion test used to identify fats and oils
• Add ethanol to the sample, shake, then pour the mixture into water.
• If fats or oils are present then a white emulsion appears at the surface.

Tests for proteins in the laboratory

Biuret test used to identify any protein
• Add dilute sodium hydroxide and dilute copper sulfate to the sample.
• A violet colour appears if a protein is present.

Quantitative tests

The above tests can be used to see if the different chemicals are present or absent. They are called qualitative tests.

They do not provide any information about how much of the chemical is present unless they are modified. One way to do this is to measure the intensity of the colour produced. This can be done with a machine called a colorimeter. It shines a light through the solution and measures how much light gets through. The lighter the colour, the more light passes through and so the less chemical is present. This is a quantitative test.

Sample questions and model answers

1 Below are the structures of two glucose molecules.

(a) Complete the equation to show how the molecules react to form a glycosidic bond and the molecule produced.

maltose   + H_2O

Remember that you will be given molecule structures. These stimulate your memory which helps you work out the answer.

(b) Which form of glucose molecules is shown? Give a reason for your answer.   [2]

α glucose, because the −OH groups on carbon atom 1 are down

The correct answer here is condensation. A regular error in questions like this is to give the wrong reaction, i.e. hydrolysis. Revise carefully then you will make the correct choice.

(c) State the type of reaction which takes place when the two molecules shown above react together.   [2]

Condensation.

2 The diagram below shows a globular protein consisting of four polypeptide chains.

Look out for similar structures in your examinations. The proteins given may be different, but the principles remain the same.

(a) Use your own knowledge and the information given to explain how this protein shows primary, secondary, tertiary and quaternary structure.   [5]

Primary structure: it is formed from chains of amino acids; it has polypeptides made of a linear sequence of amino acids.
Secondary structure: it has an α−helix, it has a β−pleated sheet.
Tertiary structure: the polypeptides are folded, the folds are held in position by disulfide bridges.
Quaternary structure: there are four polypeptides in this protein.
Two or more are bonded together to give a quaternary structure.

(b) Name and describe a test which would show that haemoglobin is a protein.   [3]

The Biuret test.
Take a sample of haemoglobin and add water, sodium hydroxide and copper sulfate.
The colour of the mixture shows as violet or mauve if the sample is a protein.

Most examinations include at least one biochemical test.

Practice examination questions

Try all of the questions and check your answers with the mark scheme on page 99

1 (a) Complete the equation below to show the breakdown of a triglyceride fat into fatty acids and glycerol. [2]

a triglyceride fat   3 molecules
of water

(b) Describe a biochemical test which would show if a sample contained fat. [3]

2 The diagram below shows a polypeptide consisting of 15 amino acids.

(a) Name the bond between each pair of amino acids in this polypeptide. [1]

(b) What is group X? [1]

(c) Which level of protein structure is shown by this polypeptide? Give a reason for your answer. [2]

Cells

The following topics are covered in this chapter:

- The ultra-structure of cells
- Isolation of cell organelles
- Specialisation of cells

2.1 The ultra-structure of cells

After studying this section you should be able to:

- *identify cell organelles and understand their roles*
- *recall the differences between prokaryotic and eukaryotic cells*

LEARNING SUMMARY

Cell organelles

AQA ▸ 1.3, 2.4

The cell is the basic functioning unit of organisms in which chemical reactions take place. These reactions involve energy release needed to support life and build structures. Organisms consist of one or more cells. The amoeba is composed of one cell, whereas millions of cells make up a human.

> **KEY POINT**
>
> Every cell possesses internal coded instructions to control cell activities and development. Cells also have the ability to continue life by some form of cell division.

Organelles are best seen with the aid of an electron microscope.

The ultra-structure of a cell can be seen using an electron microscope. Sub-cellular units called organelles become visible. Each organelle has been researched to help us understand more about the processes of life.

The animal cell and its organelles

The diagram below shows the organelles found in a typical animal cell.

A plant cell has all of the same structures plus:
- a cellulose cell wall
- chloroplasts (some cells)
- a sap vacuole with tonoplast.

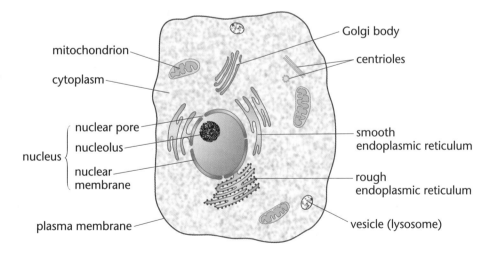

mitochondrion

cytoplasm

Golgi body

centrioles

nucleus {
nuclear pore
nucleolus
nuclear membrane

smooth endoplasmic reticulum

rough endoplasmic reticulum

plasma membrane

vesicle (lysosome)

Cell surface (plasma) membrane

This covers the outside of a cell and consists of a double layered sheet of phospholipid molecules interspersed with proteins. It separates the cell from the outside environment, gives physical protection and allows the import and export of selected chemicals.

Plasma membrane

Nucleus

This controls all cellular activity using coded instructions located in DNA. These coded instructions enable the cell to make specific proteins. RNA is produced in the nucleus and leaves via the nuclear pores. The nucleus stores, replicates and decodes DNA.

Be ready to identify all cell organelles in either a diagram or electron micrograph. A mitochondrion is often sausage shaped but the end view is circular. Look out for the internal membranes.

nucleus

nucleolus (RNA and ribosomes made here)

nuclear pore (mRNA moves out here)

cristae

mitochondrion

Mitochondria

These consist of a double membrane enclosing a semi-fluid matrix. Throughout the matrix is an internal membrane, folded into cristae. The cristae and matrix contain enzymes which enable this organelle to carry out aerobic respiration. It is the key organelle in the release of energy, making ATP available to the cell.

Mitochondria are needed for many energy requiring processes in the cell, including active transport and the movement of cilia.

Cytoplasm

Cytoplasm is often seen as grey and granular. If the image is 'clear' then you are probably looking at a vacuole.

Each organelle in a cell is suspended in a semi-liquid medium, the cytoplasm. Many ions are dissolved in it. It is the site of many chemical reactions.

Ribosomes

Look for tiny dots in the cytoplasm. They will almost certainly be ribosomes. A membrane adjacent to a line of ribosomes is probably the rough endoplasmic reticulum.

There are numerous ribosomes in a cell, located along rough endoplasmic reticulum. They aid the manufacture of proteins, being the site where mRNA meets tRNA so that amino acids are bonded together.

Endoplasmic reticulum (ER)

This is found as rough ER (with ribosomes) and smooth ER (without ribosomes). It is a series of folded internal membranes. Substances are transported in the spaces between the ER. The smooth ER aids the synthesis and transport of lipids.

ribosome

rough endoplasmic reticulum

smooth endoplasmic reticulum

Golgi body

Look for vesicles 'pinching off' the main Golgi sacs.

This is a series of flattened sacs, each separated from the cytoplasm by a membrane. The Golgi body is a packaging system where important chemicals become membrane wrapped, forming vesicles. The vesicles become detached from the main Golgi sacs, enabling the isolation of chemicals from each other in the cytoplasm. The Golgi body aids the production and secretion of many proteins, carbohydrates and glycoproteins. Vesicle membranes merge with the plasma membrane to enable secretions to take place.

Golgi body

Lysosomes

These are specialised vesicles because they contain digestive enzymes. The enzymes have the ability to break down proteins and lipids. If the enzymes were free to react in the cytoplasm then cell destruction would result.

lysosome   microvilli

Microvilli

Microvilli are small projections from the cell membrane of certain cells. They increase the surface area of the cell many times. This allows substances to be absorbed much faster across the cell membrane. Examples of cells that have microvilli are the cells lining the villi in the small intestine.

The plant cell and its organelles

All of the structures described for animal cells are also found in plant cells (except the centrioles). Additionally there are three extra structures shown in the diagram below.

> Did you spot the three extra structures in the plant cell? Remember that a root cell under the soil will not possess chloroplasts. Nor does every plant cell above the soil have chloroplasts.

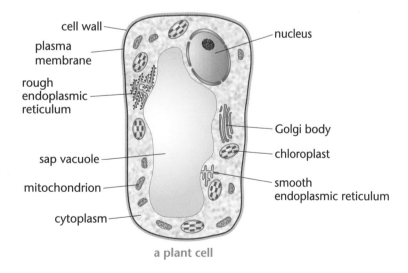

a plant cell

Cell wall

> Cells other than plant cells can have cell walls, e.g. bacteria have polysaccharides other than cellulose.

Around the plasma membrane of plant cells is the cell wall. This is secreted by the cell and consists of cellulose microfibrils embedded in a layer of calcium pectate and hemicelluloses. Between the walls of neighbouring cells calcium pectate cements one cell to the next in multi-cellular plants. Plant cell walls provide a rigid support for the cell but allow many substances to be imported or exported by the cell. The wall allows the cell to build up an effective hydrostatic skeleton. Some plant cells have a cytoplasmic link which crosses the wall. These links of cytoplasm are known as plasmodesmata.

middle lamella

plasmodesmata
(a strand of cytoplasm
connected to next cell)

plasmodesmata

outer membranes

stroma

granum
(a stack of membranes
containing chlorophyll)

thylakoid
membranes

a chloroplast

Chloroplasts

These enable the plant to photosynthesise, making glucose. Each consists of an outer covering of two membranes. Inside are more membranes stacked in piles called grana. The membranes enclose a substance vital to photosynthesis, chlorophyll. Inside the chloroplast is a matrix known as the stroma which is also involved in photosynthesis.

Sap vacuole

This is a large space in a plant cell, containing chemicals such as glucose and mineral ions in water. This solution is the sap. It is surrounded by a membrane known as the tonoplast. It is important that a plant cell contains enough water to maintain internal hydrostatic pressure. When this is achieved the cell is turgid, having maximum hydrostatic strength.

Prokaryotic and eukaryotic cells

AQA 1.3

Organisms can be classified into two groups, prokaryotic or eukaryotic according to their cellular structure.

> **KEY POINT**
> Prokaryotic cells are characteristic of two groups of organisms, bacteria and blue-green algae. Prokaryotic cells are less complex than eukaryotic ones and are considered to have evolved earlier.

The table below states similarities and differences between the two types of organism.

In an examination you will often be given a diagram of a cell from an organism you have not seen before. This is not a problem! The examiners are testing your recognition of the organelles found in typical prokaryotic and eukaryotic organisms.

		Prokaryotic cells	Eukaryotic cells
Kingdom		Prokaryotae	Protoctista, Fungi, Animalia, Plantae
Organelles	1	small ribosomes	large ribosomes
	2	DNA present but there is no nuclear membrane	DNA is enclosed in a membrane i.e. has nucleus, mitochondria, (Golgi body vesicles and ER are present)
	3	cell wall present consisting of mucopeptides	cell walls present in plant cells – cellulose cell walls present in fungi – chitin
	4	if cells have flagellae there is no 9+2 microtubule arrangement	if cells have flagellae there is a 9+2 microtubule arrangement

Progress check

1 Describe the function of each of the following cell organelles:

nucleus   Golgi body   mitochondria
ribosomes   cell (plasma) membrane

2 Give **three** structural differences between a plant and animal cell.

2 A plant cell has a cellulose cell wall, chloroplasts, and a sap vacuole lined by a tonoplast.
Cell (plasma) membrane – gives physical protection to the outside of a cell, allows the import and export of *selected* chemicals.
Golgi body – is a packaging system where chemicals become membrane wrapped, forming vesicles
ribosomes – aid the manufacture of proteins, being the site where mRNA meets tRNA so that amino acids are bonded together
mitochondria – release energy during aerobic respiration
1 nucleus – mRNA is produced in the nucleus with the help of DNA

2.2 Isolation of cell organelles

After studying this section you should be able to:

- *understand how cell fractionation and ultracentrifugation are used to isolate cell organelles*
- *understand the principles of light and electron microscopes*
- *understand how microscopic specimens are measured*

LEARNING
SUMMARY

Cell fractionation

AQA   1.3

Occasionally it is necessary to isolate organelles to investigate their structure or function, e.g. mitochondria could be used to investigate aerobic respiration away from the cell's internal environment. Cell fractionation consists of two processes: homogenisation followed by differential centrifugation. Cell fractionation depends on the different densities of the organelles.

Technique

Cells are kept:

- cool at around 5°C *(this slows down the inevitable autolysis, destruction by the cell's own enzymes)*
- in an isotonic solution, i.e. equal concentration of substances inside and outside of the cell membrane *(this ensures that the organelles are not damaged by osmosis and can still function)*
- at a specific pH by a buffer solution *(this ensures that the organelles can still function, as they are kept in suitable conditions).*

Homogenisation

The cells are homogenised in either a pestle homogeniser or a blender. This breaks the cells up releasing the organelles and cytoplasm. Many organelles are not damaged at all by this process. At this stage there is a suspension of mixed organelles.

pestle homogeniser   blender

Differential centrifugation

Equal amounts of homogenised tissue are poured into the tubes of an ultracentrifuge. This instrument spins the cell contents at a force many times greater than gravity. Organelle separation by this technique is density dependent.

First spin

The sample is spun at 600 g for 10 minutes. Nuclei, the organelles of greatest density, collect in the sediment at the base of the tube. All other cell contents are

600 g means 600 times the force of gravity. If a plant cell was centrifuged at around this speed then chloroplasts would be contained in the sediment as well as nuclei.

The principle of pouring off the supernatant to leave the pure sediment behind can be repeated at the end of each spin. In this way the main organelles can be isolated.

Note that it is much easier to obtain nuclei, because they are isolated in the first spin. Ribosomes are isolated at the final spin.

found in the supernatant (the fluid above the sediment). Pouring off the supernatant leaves the sediment of relatively pure nuclei.

Second spin

The remaining supernatant fluid is spun at 10 000 to 20 000 g for a further 20 minutes. Mitochondria, the most dense of the remaining organelles, collect in the sediment. All other cell contents are found in the supernatant.

Third spin

The remaining supernatant fluid is spun at 100 000 g for a further 60 minutes. In this sediment are fragments of endoplasmic reticulum and ribosomes. Other cell contents, e.g. cytoplasm and proteins, remain in the supernatant.

Using this technique the organelles are isolated. By providing them with suitable conditions they remain active for a time and can be used in investigations, e.g. chloroplasts given isotonic solution, suitable (warm) temperature, light, carbon dioxide and water will continue to photosynthesise.

Light and electron microscopy

AQA   1.3

Microscopes magnify the image of a specimen to enable the human eye to see minute objects not visible to the naked eye. Resolution of a microscope is the ability to distinguish between two objects as separate entities. At low resolution only one object may be detected. At high resolution two distinct objects are visible. At high resolution the image of such a specimen would show considerable detail.

The light microscope has limited resolution ($0.2\,\mu m$) due to the wavelength of light so that organelles such as mitochondria, although visible, do not have clarity. Electron microscopes have exceptional resolution. The transmission electron microscope has a high resolution (0.2 to 0.3 nm). This enables even tiny organelles to be seen.

The light microscope

This type of microscope uses white light to illuminate a specimen. The light is focused onto the specimen by a condensing lens. The specimen is placed on a microscope slide which is clipped onto a platform, known as the stage. The image is viewed via an eyepiece or ocular lens. Overall magnification of the specimen depends on the individual magnification of the eyepiece lens and objective lens. For example, if a specimen is being observed with an eyepiece × 10 and an objective lens of × 40, then the image is 400 times the true size of the specimen.

> **KEY POINT**
>
> Many specimens need staining with chemicals so that tissues and, perhaps, organelles can be seen clearly, e.g. methylene blue is used to stain nuclei. Sometimes more than one stain is used, e.g. in differential staining, so that sub-cellular parts contrast with each other.

To decide which microscope is suitable use the table below.

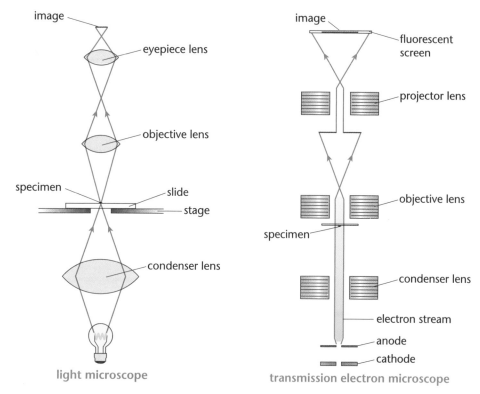

light microscope

transmission electron microscope

The electron microscope

This uses an electron stream which is directed at the specimen. The transmission electron microscope (TEM) has extremely high magnification and resolution properties. Specimens are placed in a vacuum within the microscope, to ensure the electrons do not collide with air molecules and distort the image. Stains such as osmium and uranium salts are used to make organelles distinct. These salts are absorbed by organelles and membranes differentially, e.g. the nuclear membrane absorbs more of the salts than other parts. In this way the nuclear membrane becomes more dense. When the electron beam hits the specimen, electrons are unable to pass through this dense membrane. The membrane shows up as a dark shadow area on the image, because it is in an electron shadow. Cytoplasm allows more electrons to pass through. When these electrons hit the fluorescent screen visible light is emitted. In the scanning electron microscope electrons bounce off the surface of specimens. This provides a 3D image.

Artefacts

When microscopic specimens are prepared there are often several chemical and physical procedures. Often the material is dead so changes from the living specimen are expected. Microscopic material should be analysed with care because there may have been some artificial change in the material during preparation, e.g. next to some cells a student might see a series of small circles. They look like eggs but are merely air bubbles. These are artefacts; structures alien to the material which should not be interpreted as part of the specimen.

Microscopic measurement

It is sometimes necessary to measure microscopic structures. There are two instruments needed for this process, a graticule and stage micrometer.

graticule   stage micrometer

Calibration and measurement technique

- Put a graticule into the eyepiece of a microscope.
- Look through the eyepiece lens and the graticule line can be seen.
- Put a stage micrometer on the microscope stage.
- Look through the eyepiece lens.
- Line up the ruled line of the graticule with the ruled line of the stage micrometer.
- Calibrate the eyepiece by finding out the number of eyepiece units (e.u.) equal to one stage unit (s.u.); each is 0.01 mm.
- If three eyepiece units equal 1 stage unit, then 1 eyepiece unit is equal to 0.01/3 (0.0033 mm).
- Take away the stage micrometer and replace it with a specimen.
- Measure the dimensions of the specimen in terms of eyepiece units.

> Important! Every time you change the objective lens, e.g. move from low power to high power, recalibration is necessary. In an examination this may be tested. Many candidates forget to recalibrate. Don't miss the mark!

Example

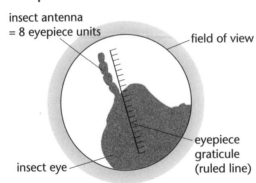

insect antenna = 8 eyepiece units

field of view

eyepiece graticule (ruled line)

insect eye

1 s.u. = 0.01 mm
3 e.u. = 1 s.u.
therefore 1 e.u. = 0.0033 mm
length of insect
antenna = 8 e.u.
= 8 × 0.0033 mm
= 0.0264 mm

2.3 Specialisation of cells

After studying this section you should be able to:

- *understand cell specialisation and how cells aggregate into tissues and organs*
- *recall a range of cell adaptations*

The earlier parts of this chapter described the structure and function of generalised animal and plant cells. Their features are found in many unicellular organisms where all the life-giving processes are carried out in one cell. Additionally many multicellular organisms exist. A few show no specialisation and consist of repeated identical cells, e.g. Volvox, a colonial alga. Most multicellular organisms exhibit specialisation, where different cells are adapted for specific roles.

Cell adaptations

Some important features:

Red blood cell
- no nucleus
- high surface area
- contains haemoglobin which has an affinity for oxygen

White blood cell (neutrophil)
- can surround foreign cells and debris
- produces enzymes to digest the foreign material

Epithelial cell (e.g. squamous cell)
- very thin
- allows exchange of chemicals

Plant palisade cell
- chloroplasts for photosynthesis
- chloroplasts can move to absorb more light
- contains chlorophyll which absorbs light
- sap vacuole stores important chemicals

Sperm cell
- flagellum for swimming
- numerous mitochondria for ATP production
- an acrosome containing enzymes to digest way into female gamete

Root hair cell
- projection of cell to increase surface area for water absorption and anchorage

Guard cell
- unevenly thickened cell walls so cells bend when turgid
- chloroplasts to provide energy for uptake of minerals and hence water.

red blood cell

neutrophil

epithelial cell

palisade, mesophyll cell of leaf

sperm cell

root hair cell

guard cells

Tissues, organs and systems

AQA ▶ 2.6

A tissue is a collection of similar cells, derived from the same source, all working together for a specific function, e.g. palisade cells of the leaf which photosynthesise or the smooth muscle cells of the intestine which carry out peristalsis.

An organ is a collection of tissues which combine their properties for a specific function, e.g. the stomach includes: smooth muscle, epithelial lining cells, connective tissue, etc. Together they enable the stomach to digest food.

A range of tissues and organs combine to form a system, e.g. the respiratory system.

In multicellular organisms specific groups of cells are specialised for a particular role. This increased efficiency helps the organism to have better survival qualities in the environment.

The photomicrograph below shows some of the cells which are part of a bone.

Haversian canal containing blood vessels and nerves

Bone cells which secrete the minerals which harden the bone

Combinations of cells each contribute their specific adaptations to the overall function of an organ. Compact bone, spongy bone and articular cartilage all have distinct but vital qualities.

Sample question and model answer

The electron micrograph below shows a lymphocyte which secretes antibodies. Antibodies are proteins.

Analyse electron micrographs carefully. Learn the typical structures of all the organelles and then you will be prepared.

(a)

(i) Name the organelles X and Y. [2]

X = nucleus
Y = mitochondrion

(ii) The cell was stained with uranium salts in preparation for a transmission electron microscope. Explain how this stain caused the nucleus to show a dark shade compared to the light shade of the cytoplasm. [4]

There are many different stains. You need to know the principle of how they work, but not specific names.

The stain was taken up by the nucleus more than the cytoplasm; the electrons could not pass through the stained (dense) parts of the nucleus so the dark nucleus parts on the screen are in electron shade. Electrons pass through the cytoplasm and cause light emission (fluorescence) at the screen.

(b)

(i) Given a piece of liver how would you isolate mitochondria from the cells? [7]

Note that there are 7 marks maximum for this question. Any 7 of the responses shown would achieve maximum credit. The ideal answer given shows 9 potential creditable points.

Put the liver in isotonic solution;
homogenise the liver or grind with a pestle and mortar;
filter the homogenate through muslin layers to remove cell debris;
put in a centrifuge; spin at 500 – 600 g for 10 minutes;
discard the pellet or sediment; centrifuge the supernatant;
spin at 10 000 – 20 000 g for 20 minutes;
mitochondria are now in the pellet or sediment.

(ii) Why is it important to keep fresh liver cells at a temperature of around 5°C during the preparation of the sample? [2]

They keep alive for a longer period since a low temperature slows down the action of the enzymes which break down the mitochondria; i.e. prevents or slows down cell autolysis (self-digestion of the cells).

37

Practice examination questions

1 The diagram shows the structure of a cell surface membrane.

    (a) Name molecules A and B. [2]

    (b) Describe one role of molecule B. [1]

    (c) Explain why the structure of molecule A means that the membrane
        forms a bilayer [2]

2 The diagram below shows an electron micrograph of a cell.

    (a) Name the parts labelled **A**, **B**, **C**, **D** and **E**. [5]

    (b) The magnification of this diagram is 10 000.
        Work out the actual diameter of the nucleus.
        Give your answer in micrometers. [3]

    (c) The cell is a liver cell. It contains many mitochondria.

    Explain why there are so many mitochondria in each liver cell. [2]

3 The diagram below shows a bacterium.

    (a) Describe **two** features, visible in the diagram, which show that the bacterium
        is a prokaryotic organism. [2]

    (b) Name **two** organelles from a human cell which show that it is a eukaryotic
        organism. [2]

4 The diagram below shows the structure of a transmission electron microscope (TEM).

image
fluorescent
screen
X
Y
specimen
condenser lens
electron stream
anode
cathode

transmission electron microscope

(a) Name lens X and lens Y.   [2]

(b) Why is it necessary for the specimen to be put in a vacuum?   [1]

(c) Occasionally an image seen when using the electron microscope shows
      an item not present in the living organism.

(i)   What name is given to this type of item?   [1]

(ii) How should the presence of the item be interpreted?   [1]

Chapter 3
Enzymes

The following topics are covered in this chapter:

- **Enzymes in action**
- **Inhibition of enzymes**
- **Enzymes and digestion**
- **Applications of enzymes**

3.1 Enzymes in action

After studying this section you should be able to:

- understand the role of the active site and the enzyme–substrate complex in enzyme action
- understand how enzymes catalyse biochemical reactions by lowering activation energy
- understand the factors which affect the rate of enzyme catalysed reactions

LEARNING SUMMARY

How enzymes work

AQA ▶ 1.1

Living cells carry out many biochemical reactions. These reactions take place **rapidly** due to the presence of enzymes. All enzymes consist of **globular proteins** which have the ability to 'drive' biochemical reactions. Some enzymes require additional non-protein groups to enable them to work efficiently, e.g. the enzyme dehydrogenase needs a coenzyme NAD to function. Most enzymes are contained within cells but some may be released and act extracellularly.

> The tertiary folding of polypeptides are responsible for the special shape of the active site.

KEY POINT

The ability of an enzyme to function depends on the specific shape of the protein molecule. The intricate shape created by polypeptide folding (see page 22) is a key factor in both theories of enzyme action.

Lock and key theory

> In an examination the lock and key theory is the most important model to consider. Remember that both catabolic and anabolic reactions may be given.

- Some part of the enzyme has a cavity with a precise shape (**active site**).
- A substrate can fit into the active site.
- The active site (lock) is exactly the correct shape to fit the substrate (key).
- The substrate binds to the enzyme forming an **enzyme–substrate complex**.
- The reaction takes place rapidly.
- Certain enzymes break a substrate down into two or more products (**catabolic** reaction).
- Other enzymes bind two or more substrates together to assemble one product (**anabolic** reaction).

> metabolic reaction = anabolic reaction + catabolic reaction
>
> Remember that metabolism is a summary of **build up** and **break down reactions**.

enzyme + substrate → enzyme–substrate complex → ready to be used again + two products have been formed

a catabolic reaction (substrate broken down)

enzyme + substrates → enzyme–substrate complex → ready to be used again + one product has been formed

an anabolic reaction (substrates used to build a new molecule)

Induced fit theory

- The active site is a cavity of a particular shape.
- Initially the active site is not the correct shape in which to fit the substrate.
- As the substrate approaches the active site, the site changes and this results in it being a perfect fit.
- After the reaction has taken place, and the products have gone, the active site returns to its normal shape.

enzyme   substrate

The shape of the active site changes as the substrate approaches.

enzyme–substrate complex

Active site is a perfect shape for the substrate.

products

Lowering of activation energy

Every reaction requires the input of energy. Enzymes reduce the level of activation energy needed as shown by the graph.

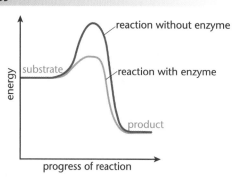

reaction without enzyme

substrate

reaction with enzyme

product

energy

progress of reaction

The higher the activation energy the slower the reaction. An enzyme reduces the amount of energy required for a biochemical reaction. When an enzyme binds with a substrate the available energy has a greater effect and the rate of catalysis increases. The conditions which exist during a reaction are very important when considering the rate of progress. Each of the following has an effect on the rate:

- concentration of substrate molecules
- concentration of enzyme molecules
- temperature
- pH.

You may be questioned on the factors which affect the rate of reaction. Less able candidates tend to remember just one or two factors. Learn all four factors here and achieve a higher grade!

What is the effect of enzyme and substrate concentration?

When considering the rate of an enzyme catalysed reaction the proportion of enzyme to substrate molecules should be considered. Every substrate molecule fits into an active site, then the reaction takes place. If there are more substrate molecules than enzyme molecules then the number of active sites available is a limiting factor. The optimum rate of reaction is achieved when all the active sites are in use. At this stage if more substrate is added, there is no increase in rate of product formation. When there are fewer substrate molecules than enzyme molecules the reaction will take place very quickly, as long as the conditions are appropriate.

Look out for questions which show the rate of reaction graphically. The examiners often test your understanding of limiting factors (see practice question on page 47).

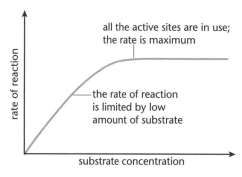

all the active sites are in use; the rate is maximum

rate of reaction

the rate of reaction is limited by low amount of substrate

substrate concentration

Remember that particles in liquids (and gases) are in constant random motion, even though we cannot see them.

How does temperature affect the rate of an enzyme catalysed reaction?

- Heat energy reaching the enzyme and substrate molecules causes them to increase random movement.
- The greater the heat energy the more the molecules move and so the more often they collide.
- The more collisions there are the greater the chance that substrates will fit into an active site, up to a specific temperature.
- At the optimum temperature of an enzyme, the reaction rate is maximum.
- Heat energy also affects the shape of the active site, the active site being the correct shape at the optimum temperature.
- At temperatures above optimum, the rate of reaction decreases because the active site begins to distort.
- Very high temperature causes the enzyme to become denatured, i.e. bonding becomes irreversibly changed and the active site is permanently damaged.
- At very high temperatures, the number of collisions is correspondingly high, but without active sites no products can be formed.
- At lower temperatures than the optimum, the rate of the reaction decreases because of reduced enzyme–substrate collisions.

Most enzymes have an optimum temperature of between 30°C and 40°C, but there are many exceptions. An example of this is shown by some bacteria that live at high temperatures in hot volcanic springs.

It is interesting to consider that some micro organisms can spoil ice-cream in a freezer whereas a different micro organism, with different enzymes, can decompose grass in a 'steaming' compost heap.

How does pH affect the rate of an enzyme catalysed reaction?

The pH of the medium can have a direct effect on the bonding responsible for the secondary and tertiary structure of enzymes. If the active site is changed then enzyme action will be affected. Each enzyme has an optimum pH.

- Many enzymes work best at neutral or slightly alkaline conditions, e.g. salivary amylase.
- Pepsin works best in acid conditions around pH 3.0, as expected considering that the stomach contains hydrochloric acid.

For the two enzyme examples above, the active sites are ideally shaped at the pHs mentioned. An inappropriate pH, often acidic, can change the active site drastically, so that the substrate cannot bind. The reaction will not take place. On most occasions the change of shape is not permanent and can be returned to optimum by the addition of an alkali.

Remember that other factors affect an enzyme catalysed reaction:
- substrate concentration
- enzyme concentration
- temperature.

Each can be a limiting factor.

Progress check

How does temperature affect the rate of the reaction by which protein is changed to polypeptides by the enzyme pepsin, in the human stomach?

$$\text{protein} \xrightarrow{\text{pepsin}} \text{polypeptides}$$

- Heat energy causes the enzyme and substrate molecules to increase random movement, increasing the chance of collision.
- At 37°C (optimum temperature) there is a greater chance that the protein will fit into an active site, so the production of polypeptides is at maximum rate.
- At 37°C (optimum temperature) the shape of the active site is best suited to fit the protein.
- At temperatures higher than 37°C the rate of reaction decreases because the active site begins to distort.
- Very high temperature causes the pepsin to become denatured, i.e. bonding has been irreversibly changed and the active site is permanently damaged.
- At very high temperatures the number of collisions is correspondingly high, but without active sites no polypeptides can be formed.
- At lower temperatures than optimum the rate of reaction decreases because of reduced enzyme–substrate collisions.

3.2 Inhibition of enzymes

After studying this section you should be able to:

- *understand the action and effects of competitive and non-competitive inhibitors*

LEARNING SUMMARY

What are inhibitors?

AQA ▶ 3.1.1

Certain chemicals can slow down or stop enzyme catalysed reactions. These chemicals are called inhibitors.

Sometimes these chemicals are substances that are naturally occurring inside cells. They may be used to regulate the rate of enzyme controlled reactions. Other inhibitors may be poisons or medicines.

Competitive inhibitors

- These are molecules of similar shape to the normal substrate and are able to bind to the active site.
- They do not react within the active site, but leave after a time without any product forming.
- The enzymic reaction is reduced because while the inhibitor is in the active site, no substrate can enter.
- Substrate molecules compete for the active site so the rate of reaction decreases.
- The higher the proportion of competitive inhibitor the slower the rate of reaction.

substrate

competitive inhibitor

the inhibitor binds with the active site

substrate cannot enter active site

substrate may now enter

Some enzymes have two sites, the active site and one other. An **allosteric** molecule fits into the alternative site. Here it changes the shape of the active site. This can stimulate the reaction if the active site becomes a better shape (**allosteric activation**). It can also inhibit if the active site becomes an inappropriate shape (**allosteric inhibition**).

Non-competitive inhibitors

- These are molecules which bind to some part of an enzyme other than the active site.
- They have a different shape to the normal substrate.
- They change the shape of the active site which no longer allows binding of the substrate.
- Some substrate molecules may reach the active site before the non-competitive inhibitor.
- The rate of reaction is reduced.
- Finally they leave their binding sites, but substrate molecules do not compete for these, so they have a greater inhibitory effect.

non-competitive inhibitor

substrate

binding site

active site has changed

substrate has opportunity to enter

The graph below shows the relative effects of competitive and non-competitive inhibitors, compared to a normal enzyme catalysed reaction.

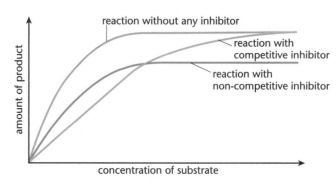

Sometimes an inhibitor will not leave the enzyme once it has bound with it. It stays permanently attached. This is called an irreversible inhibitor. Inhibitors that do leave are called reversible.

Progress check

1 Explain why a non-competitive inhibitor does not need to have the same shape as the substrate. Give a reason for your answer.

2 How does a non-competitive inhibitor reduce the rate of an enzyme catalysed reaction?

2 They change the shape of the enzyme's active site which is less suitable for the binding of the substrate, so the rate of reaction decreases.

1 No. Non-competitive inhibitors have a different shape to the normal substrate. They bind to some part of an enzyme other than the active site.

3.3 Enzymes and digestion

After studying this section you should be able to:

LEARNING SUMMARY

- recall the structure of the human digestive system
- recall the sites of secretion and action of enzymes involved in carbohydrate digestion

The human digestive system

 AQA ▶ 1.2

Humans feed heterotrophically by taking in complex organic substances. This is called ingestion. These substances are then broken down into smaller, soluble molecules by digestion.

Once digestion has occurred, the molecules can be absorbed into the blood stream. They can then be built up or assimilated into the various complex molecules that the body requires.

The human digestive system is made up of a long tube that starts at the mouth and ends at the anus. Along its length, different secretions are added to the food either from the lining of the system or from associated glands.

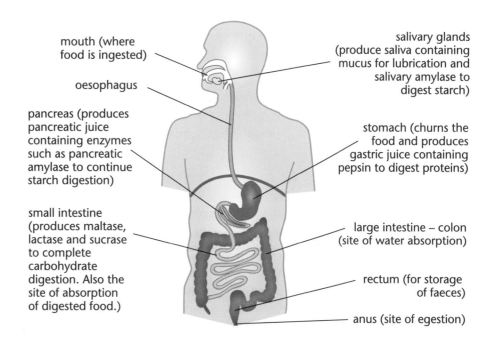

mouth (where food is ingested)

oesophagus

pancreas (produces pancreatic juice containing enzymes such as pancreatic amylase to continue starch digestion)

small intestine (produces maltase, lactase and sucrase to complete carbohydrate digestion. Also the site of absorption of digested food.)

salivary glands (produce saliva containing mucus for lubrication and salivary amylase to digest starch)

stomach (churns the food and produces gastric juice containing pepsin to digest proteins)

large intestine – colon (site of water absorption)

rectum (for storage of faeces)

anus (site of egestion)

Although different regions of the digestive system are specialised for different jobs, they are all built on a similar pattern. The diagram shows the different layers in the wall of the digestive system.

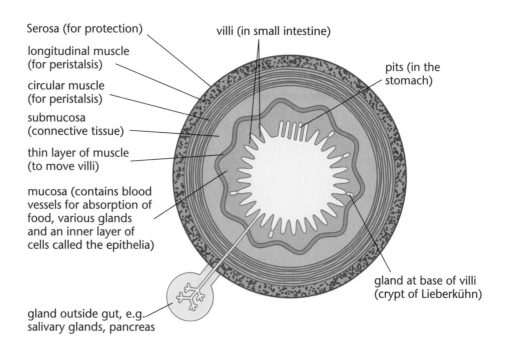

Serosa (for protection)

longitudinal muscle (for peristalsis)

circular muscle (for peristalsis)

submucosa (connective tissue)

thin layer of muscle (to move villi)

mucosa (contains blood vessels for absorption of food, various glands and an inner layer of cells called the epithelia)

gland outside gut, e.g. salivary glands, pancreas

villi (in small intestine)

pits (in the stomach)

gland at base of villi (crypt of Lieberkühn)

Digestion of carbohydrates

AQA ▸ 1.2

The human digestive enzymes are hydrolases. Each time a molecule is broken down water is required during the reaction. The table below includes some human digestive enzymes that are involved in carbohydrate digestion.

Site in alimentary canal	Secretion	Enzyme	Substrate	Product
mouth	saliva	amylase	starch	maltose
duodenum	pancreatic juice	amylase	starch	maltose
small intestine	intestinal juice	maltase	maltose	glucose
		sucrase	sucrose	glucose & fructose
		lactose	lactose	glucose & galactose

3.4 Applications of enzymes

After studying this section you should be able to:

- *describe and understand the use of lactase in producing lactose-free products*

Lactose removal from milk

AQA 1.2

We currently live in a golden age of biotechnology and enzymes are now used in a variety of applications in the home, in medicine and in industry.

Lactose removal from milk is necessary because some people have allergic reactions to lactose, the sugar in milk. **Lactase** is added to change the lactose to glucose and galactose. As a result, lactose-free milk is available to consumers.

Sample question and model answer

The graph below shows the rate of an enzyme catalysed reaction, with and without a **non-competitive inhibitor**, at different substrate concentrations.

(a) Give **one** piece of evidence from the graph which shows that the inhibitor was non-competitive rather than competitive. [1]

> A competitive inhibitor would still allow the maximum rate at high substrate concentration.

When a non-competitive inhibitor is present the maximum rate of the inhibitor-free reaction is not reached.

(b) Explain why the rates of the inhibited and non-inhibited reactions were very similar up to a substrate concentration of 20 μmol cm⁻³. [2]

> Remember that the non-competitive inhibitor binds to a different part of an enzyme and NOT the active site. It still causes a change in the active site which cannot then bind with the substrate.

Before a concentration of 20 μmol cm⁻³
- in both reactions substrate molecules are similarly successful in reaching active sites
- few inhibitor molecules have become bound to the alternative sites on the enzyme
- few active sites have been changed so are still available for the substrate.

(c) Give **two** factors that are needed to be kept constant when investigating both the inhibited and non-inhibited reactions. [2]

- temperature
- pH

Practice examination questions

1 Describe each of the following pairs to show that you understand the main differences between them:
   (a) the lock and key enzyme theory **and** the induced fit enzyme theory
   (b) reversible **and** irreversible inhibitors.   [4]

2 In terms of the tertiary structure of the enzyme, explain why amylase can break down starch but has no effect on a lipid.   [3]

3 Bacterial α-amylase works best at around 80°C.
   (a) Name the substrate which it breaks down.   [1]
   (b) Why is this enzyme described as a thermostable enzyme?   [1]

4 The diagram represents an enzyme and its substrate.

   (a) Referring to information in the diagram explain the activity of this enzyme in terms of the **induced fit theory**.   [2]
   (b) Molecule X is a non-competitive inhibitor. Explain how this inhibitor has an effect on the structure and function of the enzyme.   [3]

5 The diagram below shows a long polypeptide.

   (a) The carboxylic acid is found at one end of the polypeptide. Which group is found at the other end?   [1]
   (b) Pepsin breaks down polypeptides by breaking bonds in the centre of the molecule. This speeds up the subsequent digestion of the polypeptide. Explain how.   [2]

Chapter 4
Exchange

The following topics are covered in this chapter:

- The cell surface membrane
- The movement of molecules in and out of cells
- Gaseous exchange in humans
- Gaseous exchange in other organisms

4.1 The cell surface membrane

After studying this section you should be able to:

- *understand the importance of surface area to volume ratio*
- *recall the fluid mosaic model of the cell surface (plasma) membrane*

How important is the surface area of exchange surfaces?

AQA A   2.7

Unicellular organisms like amoeba have a very high **surface area to volume ratio**. All chemicals that are needed can pass into the cells directly and all waste can pass out efficiently. Organisms which have a high surface area to volume ratio have no need for special structures like lungs or gills.

Nutrients and oxygen passing into an organism are rapidly used up. This limits the ultimate size to which a unicellular organism can grow. If vital chemicals did not reach all parts of a cell then death would be a consequence.

A unicellular organism may satisfy all its needs by direct diffusion. However, in larger organisms cells join to adjacent ones and surfaces exposed for exchange of substances are reduced. The larger an organism the lower its surface area to volume ratio. For this reason many multicellular organisms have specially adapted exchange structures.

Fluid mosaic model of the cell surface (plasma) membrane

AQA   1.3

Ultimately the exchange of substances takes place across the cell surface membrane. This must be selective, allowing some substances in and excluding others. The cell membrane consists of a bilayer of phospholipid molecules (see page 20–21). Each phospholipid is arranged so that the hydrophilic (attracts water) head is facing towards either the cytoplasm or the outside of the cell. The hydrophobic (repels water) tails meet in the middle of the membrane. Across this expanse of phospholipids are a number of protein molecules. Some of the proteins (intrinsic) span the complete width of the membrane, some proteins (extrinsic) are partially embedded in the membrane.

Remember that plant cells have a cellulose cell wall. This gives physical support to the cell but is permeable to many molecules. Water and ions can readily pass through.

The fluid mosaic model of the cell membrane

upper surface of cell membrane protein

phospholipid head

outside of cell

protein channel to transport specific substances into cell

phospholipid bilayer

inside of cell

protein molecule

hydrophobic tail
hydrophilic head

phospholipid molecule

Functions of cell membrane molecules

The term 'fluid mosaic' was given to the cell membrane because of the dynamic nature of the component molecules of the membrane. Many of the proteins seem to 'float' through an apparent 'sea' of phospholipids. Few molecules are static. The fluidity of the membrane is controlled by the quantity of cholesterol molecules. These are found inbetween the tails of the phospholipids.

Phospholipid

Small lipid-soluble molecules pass through the membrane easily because they dissolve as they pass through the phospholipid's bilayer. Small uncharged molecules also pass through the bilayer.

small lipid-soluble molecules pass through

Channel proteins (ion gates)

Larger molecules and charged molecules can pass through the membrane due to channel proteins. Some are adjacent to a receptor protein, e.g. at a synapse a transmitter substance binds to a receptor protein. This opens the channel protein or ion gate and sodium ions flow in.

Not all channel proteins need a receptor protein.

transmitter substance

receptor protein

Na⁺   ion gate open

Na⁺

> When the molecule binds to a receptor molecule it is similar to a substrate binding with an enzyme's active site. On this occasion the receptor site is the correct shape.

Carrier protein molecule

Some molecules which approach a cell may bind with a carrier protein. This has a site which the incoming molecule can bind to. This causes a change of shape in the carrier protein which deposits the molecule into the cell cytoplasm.

once in position the molecule changes the shape of the carrier protein

the site gives up the molecule on the inside of the cell

carrier protein

Recognition proteins

These are extrinsic proteins, some having carbohydrate components, which help in cell recognition (cell signalling) and cell interaction, e.g. foreign protein on a bacterium would be recognised by white blood cells and the cell would be attacked. The combination of a

carbohydrate

recognition protein

> White blood cells continually check the proteins on cell membranes. Those recognised as 'self' are not attacked, whereas those which are not 'self' are attacked.

protein with a carbohydrate is called a glycoprotein. The carbohydrate chains are only on the outside of the cell membrane and are called the glycocalyx.

> **KEY POINT**
>
> The cell surface membrane is the key structure which forms a barrier between the cell and its environment. Nutrients, water and ions must enter and waste molecules must leave. Equally important is the exclusion of dangerous chemicals and inclusion of vital cell contents. It is no surprise that the cell makes further compartments within the cell using membranes of similar structure to the cell surface membrane. High temperatures can destroy the structure of the cell membrane and then it loses its ability to contain the cell contents.

4.2 The movement of molecules in and out of cells

After studying this section you should be able to:

- understand the range of methods by which molecules cross cell membranes
- understand the processes of diffusion, facilitated diffusion, osmosis and active transport

How do substances cross the cell surface membrane?

AQA 1.3

Cells need to obtain substances vital in sustaining life. Some cells secrete useful substances but all cells excrete waste substances. There are several mechanisms by which molecules move across the cell surface membrane.

Diffusion

Note that diffusion is the movement of molecules down a concentration gradient.

Molecules in liquids and gases are in constant random motion. When different concentrations are in contact, the molecules move so that they are in equal concentration throughout. An example of this is when sugar is put into a cup of tea. If left, sugar molecules will distribute themselves evenly, even without stirring. Diffusion is the movement of molecules from where they are in high concentration to where they are in low concentration. Once evenly distributed the *net* movement of molecules stops.

Factors which affect the rate of diffusion

- Surface area.
  the greater the surface area the greater the rate of diffusion
- The difference in concentration on either side of the membrane.
  the greater the difference the greater the rate
- The size of molecules.
  smaller molecules may pass through the membrane faster than larger ones
- The presence of pores in the membrane.
  pores can speed up diffusion
- The width of the membrane.
  the thinner the membrane the faster the rate.

Sometimes the membrane is stated as being selectively permeable, partially permeable or semi-permeable. They all mean the same thing.

Facilitated diffusion

This is a special form of diffusion in which protein carrier molecules are involved. It is much faster than regular diffusion because of the carrier molecules. Each carrier will only bind with a specific molecule. Binding changes the shape of the carrier which then deposits the molecule into the cytoplasm. No energy is used in the process.

selectively permeable membrane

A   B

◦ water molecule
◯ solute molecule

water molecules move from B to A

Osmosis

This is the movement of water molecules across a selectively permeable membrane:

- from a lower concentrated solution to a higher concentrated solution
- from where water molecules are at a higher concentration to where they are at a lower concentration
- from a hypotonic solution to a hypertonic solution
- from a hyperosmotic solution to a hypo-osmotic solution
- from an area of higher water potential to lower water potential.

The diagram on the left shows a model of osmosis.

Remember that osmosis is about the movement of **water molecules**. No other substance moves!

What is the relationship between water potential of the cell and the concentration of an external solution?

The term 'water potential' is used as a measure of water movement from one place to another in a plant. It is measured in terms of pressure and the units are either kPa (kilopascals) or MPa (megapascals). Water potential is indicated by the symbol ψ *(pronounced psi)*. The following equation allows us to work out the water 'status' of a plant cell.

ψ (cell) water potential (of cell)	=	ψs solute potential (of ions inside cell)	+	ψp pressure potential (of cell wall)	K E Y P O I N T

> Remember that water moves from an area of higher water potential to an area of lower water potential. When a cell at −4 MPa is next to a cell at the less negative value the water moves to the more negative value, i.e. −4 MPa > −6 MPa

concentration of solution outside cell increases

> Note that pressure potential only has a value **above** zero when the cell membrane **begins** to contact the cell wall. The greater the pressure potential the more the cell wall resists water entry. At turgidity ψs = ψp when net water movement is zero.

total plasmolysis
- vacuole has almost disappeared
- minimum hydrostatic pressure
- also known as flaccid

incipient plasmolysis
- cell membrane begins to leave the cell wall as water is lost

full turgidity
- vacuole maximum volume
- no more water can enter
- maximum hydrostatic pressure
- cell membrane is forced against the cell wall

Active transport

> Note that active transport is the movement of molecules up a concentration gradient.

In active transport molecules move from where they are in lower concentration to where they are in higher concentration. A protein carrier molecule is used. This is against the concentration gradient and always needs energy. A plant may contain a higher concentration of Mg^{2+} ions than the soil. It obtains a supply by active transport through the cell surface membranes of root hairs. Only Mg^{2+} ions can bind with the specific protein carrier molecules responsible for their entry into the plant. This is also known as active ion uptake, but is a form of active transport. Any process that reduces respiration in cells will reduce active transport, e.g. adding a poison such as cyanide or reducing oxygen availability. This is because energy is needed for the process and this energy is released by respiration.

In the small intestine, glucose is absorbed into the bloodstream indirectly by active transport. Sodium ions are pumped out of the epithelial cells allowing glucose and sodium ions to diffuse into the cell by a co-transporter system.

Endocytosis, exocytosis, pinocytosis and phagocytosis

endocytosis

vacuole

Some substances, often due to their large size, enter cells by endocytosis as follows:

- the substance contacts the cell surface membrane which indents
- the substance is surrounded by the membrane, forming a vacuole or vesicle
- each vacuole contains the substance and an outer membrane which has detached from the cell surface membrane.

When fluids enter the cell in this way this is known as pinocytosis. When the substances are large solid particles, this is called phagocytosis. Some substances leave the cell in a reverse of endocytosis. Here the membrane of the vacuole or vesicle merges with the cell surface membrane depositing its contents into the outside environment of the cell. This is known as exocytosis.

Progress check

1 A plant contains a greater concentration of Fe^{2+} ions than the soil in which it is growing. Name and describe the process by which the plant absorbs the ions against the concentration gradient.

2 Explain the following:
   (a) Endocytosis of an antigen by a phagocyte
   (b) Exocytosis of amylase molecules from a cell.

1 **Active transport:** molecules move from a lower concentration to a higher concentration; through the cell surface membranes of root hairs; protein carrier molecules in membranes; energy needed; Fe^{2+} ions can bind with the protein carrier molecules which allow entry into the plant.

2 (a) **Endocytosis:** antigen contacts the cell membrane of the phagocyte; cell membrane surrounds the antigen, forming a vacuole; the vacuole contains the antigen and an outer membrane which has detached from the cell surface membrane.
   (b) **Exocytosis:** a vesicle in the cell contains amylase molecules; the vesicle merges with the cell membrane; amylase contents deposited outside of the cell.

4.3 Gaseous exchange in humans

After studying this section you should be able to:

- *understand why organisms need to be adapted for gaseous exchange*
- *explain how the human breathing system brings about ventilation and gaseous exchange*

LEARNING SUMMARY

How are organisms adapted for efficient gaseous exchange?

AQA   1.4, 2.7

The range of respiratory surfaces in this chapter each have common properties, such as high surface area to volume ratio, one cell thick lining tissue, many capillaries.

The exchange of substances across cell surface membranes has been described. Larger organisms have a major problem in exchange because of their low surface area to volume ratio. Some organisms, like flatworms, have a large surface area due to the shape of their body. Other organisms satisfy their needs by having tissues and organs which have special adaptations for efficient exchange. In simple terms, these structures achieve a very high surface area, e.g. a leaf, and link to the transport system to allow import and export from the organ.

Gaseous exchange in humans

AQA 1.4

You should be aware of the effects of smoking (p90), TB (p93), fibrosis, asthma and emphysema on the function of the lungs.

The diagram below shows the human gas exchange system. The alveoli are the site of gaseous exchange and they are connected to the outside air via a system of branching tubes.

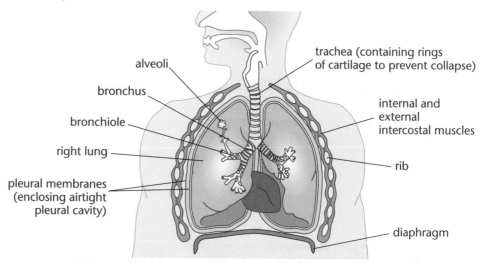

Ventilation

Drawing air in and out of the lungs involves changes in pressure and volume in the chest. These changes work because the pleural membranes form an airtight pleural cavity.

Breathing in (inhaling):
1. The external intercostal muscles contract, moving the ribs upwards and outwards.
2. The diaphragm contracts and flattens.
3. Both of these actions will increase the volume in the pleural cavity and so decrease the pressure.
4. Air is therefore drawn into the lungs.

Breathing out (exhaling):
1. The internal intercostal muscles relax and the ribs move down and inwards.
2. The diaphragm relaxes and domes upwards.
3. The volume in the pleural cavity is decreased so the pressure is increased.
4. Air is forced out of the lungs.

Lungs of a mammal

The ventilation mechanism allows inhalation of air, which then diffuses into alveoli to exchange the respiratory gases. Completion of ventilation takes place when gases are expelled into the atmosphere. The diagram on the left shows the structure of the alveoli.

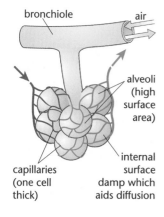

Adaptations of lungs for gaseous exchange

- Air flows through a trachea (windpipe) supported by cartilage.
- It reaches the alveoli via tubes known as bronchi and bronchioles.
- Lungs have many alveoli (air sacs) which have a high surface area.
- Each alveolus is very thin (diffusion is faster over a short distance).
- Each alveolus has an inner film of moisture containing a chemical called surfactant. This reduces the surface tension and makes it easier to inflate the lungs.
- Each alveolus has many capillaries, each one cell thick, to aid diffusion.
- There are many blood vessels in the lungs to give a high surface area for gaseous exchange and transport of respiratory substances.

Measuring ventilation

The process of ventilation can be investigated using a device called a spirometer. It can measure the volume of air exchanged in a single breath. This is called the tidal volume. It can also measure the number of breaths per minute – the breathing rate. If these two figures are multiplied together, the result gives the volume of gas exchanged in one minute, the pulmonary ventilation.

pulmonary ventilation   =   tidal volume   ×   breathing rate

4.4 Gaseous exchange in other organisms

After studying this section you should be able to:

- *recall where gaseous exchange occurs in a dicotyledonous leaf, the gills of a bony fish and the tracheal system of an insect*
- *show awareness of the adaptations of leaves, gills and tracheoles for efficient gaseous exchange*

A dicotyledonous leaf

AQA   2.7

The diagram below shows a section through a leaf. Leaves of plants give a high surface area over which exchange takes place. Specialised tissues increase the efficiency of exchange to allow photosynthesis to supply the plant with enough energy-rich carbohydrates.

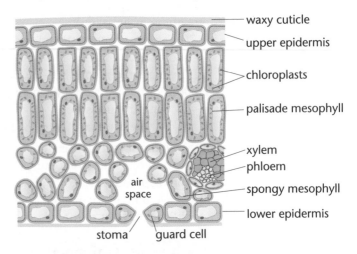

- waxy cuticle
- upper epidermis
- chloroplasts
- palisade mesophyll
- xylem
- phloem
- spongy mesophyll
- lower epidermis

air space

stoma   guard cell

Adaptations of a leaf for photosynthesis

- A flat, thin blade (lamina) to allow maximum light absorption.
- Cells of the upper epidermis have a waxy cuticle to reflect excess light but allow entry of enough light for photosynthesis.
- Each leaf has many chloroplasts to absorb a maximum amount of light.
- Chloroplasts contain many thylakoid membranes, stacked in grana to give a high surface area to absorb the maximum quantity of light.
- Palisade cells, containing chloroplasts, pack closely together to 'capture' the maximum amount of light.
- Many guard cells open stomata to allow carbon dioxide in and oxygen out during photosynthesis.

- Air spaces in the mesophyll store lots of carbon dioxide for photosynthesis or lots of oxygen for respiration.
- Xylem of the vascular bundles brings water to the leaf for photosynthesis.
- Phloem takes the carbohydrate away from the leaf after photosynthesis.

The gills of a bony fish

AQA   2.7

gill arch

gill lamella (or primary lamella)

gill plate (or secondary lamella)

direction of blood flow

water current

The ventilation mechanism of a fish allows intake of water, and passes it across the gills. The diagram on the left shows the structures of the gills which allow maximum exchange to take place.

Adaptations of gills for gaseous exchange

- The gills of a bony fish have a very high surface area to volume ratio.
- Gills consist of many flat gill filaments, stacked on top of each other, to give a high surface area for maximum exchange.
- Each gill filament has many gill plates which further increase surface area.
- Gill plates are very thin and full of blood capillaries to aid exchange.
- The gradients of O_2 and CO_2 are kept at a maximum by the counter-current flow mechanism. By allowing water to flow over the gills in an opposite direction to blood, maximum diffusion rate is achieved.

All respiratory surfaces are damp to allow effective transport across cell membranes.

Progress check

Describe and explain how the gills of a bony fish are adapted for efficient gaseous exchange.

Each gill consists of many thin gill filaments, stacked on top of each other which give a high surface area to volume ratio, for maximum exchange of gases; each gill filament has many gill plates which further increase surface area; each gill plate is very thin and full of blood capillaries; the gradients of O_2 and CO_2 are kept at a maximum by counter-current flow; water flows over the gills in an opposite direction to blood to achieve maximum diffusion rates.

The tracheal system of insects

AQA   2.7

An insect is covered by an exoskeleton which is covered in wax and is impermeable. Insects have a series of holes in the cuticle called spiracles. These spiracles lead into a set of tubes called the tracheal system. The larger tubes, called tracheae, branch into smaller tubes called tracheoles. These tiny tubes are permeable and end on the cells of the body. Oxygen can therefore diffuse from the air into the cells. This system helps reduce water loss from the insect.

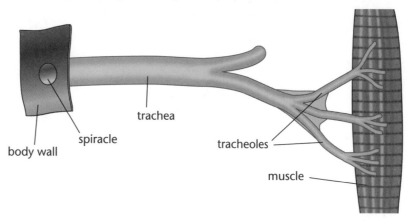

body wall

spiracle

trachea

tracheoles

muscle

Sample question and model answer

The diagram below shows two adjacent plant cells A and B.
The water potential equation is:

$$\psi(cell) = \psi s + \psi p$$

cell A   cell B

(a) (i) Calculate the water potential of cell B.   [1]

> Using the equation:
> $\psi (cell) = \psi s + \psi p$
> $= -8$ MPa $+ 3$ MPa
> $= -5$ MPa

In this question you were given the equation. Try to remember it because it could earn you a mark. Additionally, if there were calculations you need the equation to access the other marks.

When given any two of the values you can work out the other.

(ii) Draw an arrow on the diagram to show the direction of water flow. Show how you worked out the direction.   [2]

> The arrow should be drawn from cell B to cell A.
> Direction from -5 MPa to -10 MPa.

(iii) What is the value of the pressure potential (ψp) of cell A?   [1]

> $\psi (cell) = \psi s + \psi p,$
> -10 MPa $= -10$ MPa $+ \psi p$
> $\psi p = -10$ MPa $+ 10$ MPa
> $= 0$ MPa

Note that from total plasmolysis up to incipient plasmolysis the resistance of the cell, i.e. ψp is zero.

Only when the cell membrane contacts with the wall does it have an effect.

(iv) Name the condition of the cell when $\psi(cell) = 0$ [1]

> full turgor or fully turgid

(b) Give **one** difference between the following terms: [2]

facilitated diffusion

> molecules move down a gradient

active transport

> energy is needed for the process

Be careful with this type of question. You may believe that 'up a gradient' could be given for active transport. It is correct, but it's too close to the 'down a gradient' idea for facilitated diffusion.

Go for a completely different idea, as shown.

(c) What effect would the following temperatures have on the active transport of Mg^{2+} ions across a cell surface membrane of a plant cell? Assume the plant is a British native.   [4]

(i) 30°C

> It is likely that active transport would be efficient because the temperature would be ideal for the Mg^{2+} to bind with a carrier molecule.

(ii) 80°C

> process likely not to work;
> protein carrier denatured;
> Mg^{2+} would not be able to bind.

1

cell A   cell B   cell C

Cells A, B and C have been placed in different concentrations of salt solution.

(a) Explain each of the following in terms of water potential.

   (i) Cell A did not change size at all.

   (ii) Cell B decreased in volume.

   (iii) Cell C became swollen and burst. [3]

(b) Which process is responsible for the changes to cells B and C? [1]

2 (a) Give one similarity between active transport and facilitated diffusion. [1]

  (b) Give one difference between active transport and facilitated diffusion. [1]

3 The diagram shows a section through a leaf.

thick waxy cuticle
upper epidermis
chloroplast
mesophyll
palisade cell
spongy cell
lower epidermis
hairs
stoma   guard cell

Describe how the leaf is adapted for efficient photosynthesis. [6]

4 Describe and explain how the following are adapted to efficient gaseous exchange.

(a) The alveoli of lungs. [4]

(b) The gills of a fish. [4]

Transport

The following topics are covered in this chapter:

- *Mass transport systems*
- *Heart: structure and function*
- *Blood vessels*

- *The transport of substances in the blood*
- *The transport of substances in a plant*

5.1 Mass transport systems

After studying this section you should be able to:

LEARNING SUMMARY

- *explain why most multicellular organisms need a mass transport system*
- *understand the importance of a high surface area to volume ratio*

Why do most multicellular organisms need a mass transport system?

AQA 2.7

The bigger an organism is, the lower its surface area to volume ratio. Substances needed by a large organism could not be supplied through its exposed external surface. Oxygen passing through an external surface would be rapidly used up before reaching the many layers of underlying cells. Similarly waste substances would not be excreted quickly enough. This problem has been solved, through evolution, by specially adapted tissues and organs.

> **KEY POINT**
>
> Leaves, roots, gills and lungs all have high surface area to volume properties so that supplies of substances vital to all the living cells are made available by these structures. Movement of substances to and from these structures is carried out by efficient mass transport systems.

This is a little like transport on trains where people travel together on the same train, in the same direction, at the same speed, but may get off at different places.

In a mass transport system, all the substances move in the same direction at the same speed. Across the range of multicellular organisms found in the living world are a number of mass transport systems, e.g. the mammalian circulatory system and the vascular system of a plant.

Mass transport systems are just as important for the rapid removal of waste as they are for supplies. Supplies include an immense number of substances, e.g. glucose, oxygen and ions. Even communication from one cell to another can take place via a mass transport system, e.g. hormones in a blood stream.

The greater the metabolic rate of an organism, the greater the demands on its mass transport system.

5.2 Heart: structure and function

After studying this section you should be able to:

- *recall the structure, cardiac cycle and electrical stimulation of a mammalian heart*

LEARNING SUMMARY

The mammalian heart

AQA ▶ 1.5

The heart consists of a range of tissues. The most important one is cardiac muscle. The cells have the ability to contract and relax through the complete life of the person, without ever becoming fatigued. Each cardiac muscle cell is myogenic. This means it has its own inherent rhythm. Below are diagrams of the heart and its position in the circulatory system.

Note that tricuspid and bicuspid valves are known as atrioventricular valves.

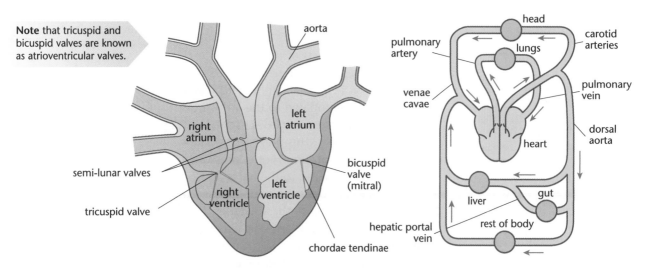

Structure

The heart consists of four chambers, right and left atria above right and left ventricles. The functions of each part are as follows.

If blood moved in the wrong direction, then transport of important substances would be impeded.

- The **right atrium** links to the **right ventricle** by the **tricuspid valve**. This valve prevents backflow of the blood into the atrium above, when the ventricle contracts.
- The **left atrium** links to the **left ventricle** by the **bicuspid valve (mitral valve)**. This also prevents backflow of the blood into the atrium above.
- The **chordae tendonae** attach each ventricle to its **atrioventricular valve**. Contractions of the ventricles have a tendency to force these valves up into the atria. Backflow of blood would be dangerous, so the chordae tendonae hold each valve firmly to prevent this from occurring.

Check out these diagrams of a valve.

You can work out if a valve is open or closed in terms of pressure. Higher pressure above than below a semi-lunar valve closes it. Higher pressure below the semi-lunar valve than above, opens it.

- Semi-lunar (pocket) valves are found in the blood vessels leaving the heart (pulmonary artery and aorta). They only allow exit of blood from the heart through these vessels following ventricular contractions. Elastic recoil of these arteries and relaxation of the ventricles closes each semi-lunar valve.
- Ventricles have thicker muscular walls than atria. When each atrium contracts it only needs to propel the blood a short distance into each ventricle.
- The left ventricle has even thicker muscular walls than the right ventricle. The left ventricle needs a more powerful contraction to propel blood to the systemic circulation (all of the body apart from the lungs). The right ventricle propels blood to the nearby lungs. The contraction does not need to be so powerful.

Cardiac cycle

Blood must continuously be moved around the body, collecting and supplying vital substances to cells as well as removing waste from them. The heart acts as a pump using a combination of systole (contractions) and diastole (relaxation) of the chambers. The cycle takes place in the following sequence.

Stage 1

Ventricular diastole, atrial systole

Both ventricles relax simultaneously. This results in lower pressure in each ventricle compared to each atrium above. The atrioventricular valves open partially. This is followed by the atria contracting which forces blood through the atrioventricular valves. It also closes the valves in the vena cava and pulmonary vein. This prevents backflow of blood.

semi-lunar valves are closed

atrioventricular valves are open

Stage 2

Ventricular systole, atrial diastole

Both atria then relax. Both ventricles contract simultaneously. This results in higher pressure in the ventricles compared to the atria above. The difference in pressure closes each atrioventricular valve. This prevents backflow of blood into each atrium. Higher pressure in the ventricles compared to the aorta and pulmonary artery opens the semi-lunar valves and blood is ejected into these arteries. So blood flows through the systemic circulatory system via the aorta and vena cava and through the lungs via the pulmonary vessels.

Stage 3

Ventricular diastole, atrial diastole

Immediately following ventricular systole, both ventricles and atria relax for a short time. Higher pressure in the aorta and pulmonary artery than in the ventricles closes the semi-lunar valves. This prevents the backflow of blood. Higher pressure in the vena cava and pulmonary vein than in the atria results in the refilling of the atria.

The cycle is now complete – *GO BACK TO STAGE 1!*

The whole sequence above is one cardiac cycle or heartbeat and it takes less than one second. The number of heartbeats per minute varies to suit the activity of an organism. Vigorous exercise is accompanied by an increase in heart rate to allow faster collection, supply and removal of substances because of enhanced blood flow. Conversely during sleep, at minimum metabolic rate, heart rate is correspondingly low because of minimum requirements by the cells.

Examination questions often test your knowledge of the opening and closing of valves. Always analyse the different pressures given in the question. A greater pressure behind a valve opens it. A greater pressure in front closes it.

Returning to Stage 1, the cycle begins again. The hormone adrenaline increases the heart rate still further. Even your examinations may increase your heart rate!

How is the heart rate controlled?

It has already been stated that the cardiac muscle cells have their own inherent rhythm. Even an individual cardiac muscle cell will contract and relax on a microscope slide under suitable conditions. An orchestra would not be able to play music in a coordinated way without a conductor. The cardiac muscle cells must be

SAN

AVN

Purkinje tissue

The SAN is the natural pacemaker of the heart.

All of the Purkinje fibres together are known as the **Bundle of His**.

This is one of the examiners' favourite ways to test heart-related concepts. Look at the **peak** of the **ventricular contraction**. It coincides with the **trough** in the **ventricular volume**. This is not surprising, because as the ventricle contracts it empties! Use the data of higher pressure in one part and lower in another to explain:

(a) movement of blood from one area to another
(b) the closing of valves.

similarly coordinated, by a pacemaker area in the heart. Electrical stimulation from the brain can alter the activity of the pacemaker and therefore change the rate and strength of the heartbeat.

- The heart control centre in the brain is in the medulla oblongata.
- The sympathetic nerve stimulates an increase in heart rate.
- The vagus nerve stimulates a decrease in heart rate.
- These nerves link to a pacemaker structure in the wall of the right atrium, the sinoatrial node (SAN).
- A wave of electrical excitation moves across both atria.
- They respond by contracting (the right one slightly before the left).
- The wave of electrical activity reaches a second pacemaker, the atrioventricular node (AVN), which conducts the electrical activity through the Purkinje fibres.
- These Purkinje fibres pass through the septum of the heart deep into the walls of the left and right ventricles.
- The ventricle walls begin to contract from the apex (base) upwards.
- This ensures that blood is ejected efficiently from the ventricles.

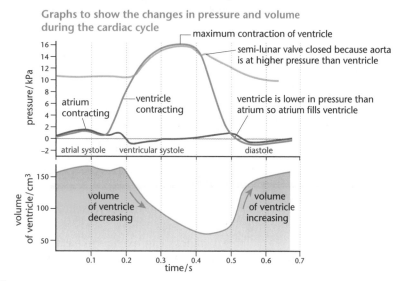

Graphs to show the changes in pressure and volume during the cardiac cycle

Cardiac output

The cardiac output is the volume of blood that is pumped out by one of the ventricles in a minute. It can be worked out using the formula:

Cardiac Output = Stroke Volume x Heart Rate
(volume of blood pumped out per beat by one ventricle)

Progress check

The medulla oblongata can increase the heart rate. The statements below include all of the events which take place, but in the wrong order. Write them out in the correct sequence.

A this ensures that blood is ejected efficiently from the ventricles

B the wave of electrical activity reaches the **atrioventricular node (AVN)** which conducts the electrical activity through the **Purkinje fibres**

C a wave of electrical excitation moves across both atria

D the sympathetic nerve conducts electrical impulses

E electrical impulses are received at the **sinoatrial node (SAN)**

F as a result the atria contract

G the ventricle walls begin to contract from the apex (base) upwards

D E C F B G A

5.3 Blood vessels

After studying this section you should be able to:

- *describe the structure and functions of arteries, capillaries and veins*
- *understand the importance of valves in the return of blood to the heart*
- *understand the difference between plasma, tissue fluid and lymph*

Arteries, veins and capillaries

AQA 2.7

The blood is transported to the tissues via the vessels. The main propulsion is by the ventricular contractions. Blood leaves the heart via the arteries, reaches the tissues via the capillaries, then returns to the heart via the veins. Each blood vessel has a space through which the blood passes; this is the lumen. The structure of the vessels is shown below.

Artery

Note that the pressure in the **arteries** is highest because:

(a) they are closest to the ventricles
(b) they contract forcefully themselves.

Capillaries are the next highest in pressure, the main factor being their resistance to blood flow.

Finally, the pressure of **veins** is the lowest because:

(a) they are furthest from the ventricles
(b) they have a low amount of muscle.

If given blood pressures of vessels, be ready to predict the correct direction of blood flow.

- It has a thick tunica externa which is an outer covering of tough collagen fibres.
- It has a tunica media which is a middle layer of smooth muscle and elastic fibres.
- It has a lining of squamous endothelium (very thin cells).
- It can contract using its thick muscular layer.

tunica (collagen externa fibres)
lumen
tunica media
endothelial lining

Capillary

- It is a very thin blood vessel, the endothelium is just one cell thick.
- Substances can exchange easily.
- It has such a high resistance to blood flow that blood is slowed down. This gives more time for efficient exchange of chemicals at the tissues.

endothelium
lumen

Vein

- It has a thin tunica externa which is an outer covering of tough collagen fibres.
- It has a very thin tunica media which is a middle layer of smooth muscle and elastic fibres.
- It has a lining of squamous endothelium (very thin cells).
- It is lined with semi-lunar valves which prevent the backflow of blood.

tunica externa (collagen fibres)
lumen
tunica media
endothelial lining

How do the veins return the blood to the heart?

Veins have a thin tunica media, so only mild contractions are possible. They return blood in an unexpected way. Every time the organism moves physically, blood is squeezed between skeletal muscles and forced along the vein.

direction of blood flow

semi-lunar valve

> Blood must travel towards the heart because of the direction of the semi-lunar valves. Any attempt at backflow and the semi-lunar valves shut tightly!

Capillary network

Every living cell needs to be close to a capillary. The arteries transport blood from the heart but before entry into the capillaries it needs to pass through smaller vessels called arterioles. Many arterioles contain a ring of muscle known as a pre-capillary sphincter. When this is contracted the constriction shuts off blood flow to the capillaries, but when it is dilated, blood passes through. Some capillary networks have a shunt vessel. When the sphincter is constricted blood is diverted along the shunt vessel so the capillary network is by-passed. After the capillary network has permeated an organ the capillaries link into a venule which joins a vein.

> In the skin the superficial capillaries have the arteriole/shunt vessel/venule arrangement as shown opposite. When the arteriole is dilated (**vasodilation**) more heat can be lost from the skin. When the arteriole is constricted (**vasoconstriction**) the blood cannot enter the capillary network so is diverted to the core of the body. Less heat is lost from the skin.

Although the pressure of the blood in the capillaries is lower than in the arteries or arterioles, there is still enough pressure to force out some of the liquid part of the blood. The liquid part of the blood is called plasma and when it is forced out of the capillaries it is called tissue fluid.

This tissue fluid bathes the cells, supplying them with nutrients and taking up waste products. At the venous end of the capillary bed, most of this tissue fluid is reabsorbed back into the capillaries.

Lymphatic system

There is a network of vessels other than the blood system. They are the lymphatic vessels. They collect any tissue fluid that is not reabsorbed back into the capillaries.

The lymph vessels have valves to ensure transport is in one direction. Along some parts of the lymphatic system are lymph nodes. These are swellings lined with white blood cells (macrophages and lymphocyte cells). The lymph fluid is finally emptied back into the blood near the heart.

Progress check

The diagram shows the structure of a blood vessel.

(a) (i) Which type of vessel, artery, vein or capillary is shown? Give a reason for your choice.

(ii) What is the function of the tunica media?

(b) The pressure values 30 kPa, 10 kPa and 5 kPa correspond to the different types of vessel. Give the correct value for each vessel so that blood flows around the body.

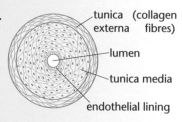

(b) artery, 30 kPa, capillary, 10 kPa and vein, 5 kPa.

(ii) contracts to help transport blood.

(a) (i) artery; the vessel has a thick tunica externa

5.4 The transport of substances in the blood

LEARNING SUMMARY

After studying this section you should be able to:

- describe the transport of oxygen in the blood and explain how oxygen is released at the tissues

How is oxygen transported?

AQA ▶ 2.4

Oxygen is absorbed in the lungs from fresh air which has been breathed in. Red blood cells (erythrocytes) contain the protein haemoglobin which can reversibly combine with oxygen. In the lungs, where the concentration of oxygen is high, haemoglobin will take up oxygen and form oxyhaemoglobin. In the tissues where the oxygen concentration is low, the oxyhaemoglobin will dissociate and release the oxygen. This is shown by the graph below which is called the oxygen dissociation curve.

Features of the dissociation curve

- At high partial pressures of oxygen, haemoglobin has a high affinity (attraction) for oxygen and is highly saturated.
- At low partial pressures, the affinity is lower and the oxyhaemoglobin dissociates and is less saturated.
- The curve is sigmoid or 'S' shaped. This means that the curve is steep and a small change in partial pressure causes a massive loading or unloading of oxygen.

Changes to the dissociation curve

Different factors can cause changes to the dissociation curve:

- The greater the amount of carbon dioxide at the tissues, the more the dissociation curve is moved to the right, and the more oxygen is 'off-loaded' to the tissues. This is called the Bohr shift. The carbon dioxide lowers the affinity of the haemoglobin for oxygen.

- Fetal haemoglobin has a greater affinity for oxygen than adult haemoglobin. This allows the fetus to take oxygen from the mother's haemoglobin.

Myoglobin

Myoglobin only has one polypeptide chain compared to four found in each molecule of haemoglobin. Myoglobin is often found in diving animals or animals that live in anaerobic mud, e.g. lugworms.

There is another substance that can act as a respiratory pigment. This is myoglobin. It does not travel in the blood but is found in muscle. It has a greater affinity for oxygen than haemoglobin and so only releases oxygen at very low partial pressures. It acts as a store of oxygen trying to prevent anaerobic respiration from occurring.

5.5 The transport of substances in a plant

After studying this section you should be able to:

- *recall the structure of a root and understand how water and ions are absorbed*
- *recall the structure of xylem and phloem and explain the processes by which they transport essential chemicals*
- *understand how plants lose water and how this loss can be measured*
- *recall the adaptations of xerophytes*

LEARNING SUMMARY

Root structure and functions

AQA   2.7

The roots of a green plant need to exchange substances with the soil environment. The piliferous zone just behind a root tip has many root hairs which have a high surface area to volume ratio.

- Root hairs are used for absorption of water and mineral ions and the excretion of carbon dioxide.

Note that the root hairs also absorb oxygen from the air to aid aerobic respiration. The high surface area to volume ratio certainly helps!

- They have a cell membrane with a high surface area to volume ratio to efficiently absorb water, mineral ions and oxygen, and excrete carbon dioxide.

- They project out into the soil particles which are surrounded by soil water at high water potential compared with the low water potential of the contents of the root hairs.

Remember that water moves from a higher water potential to a more negative water potential.

- They have a cell membrane which is partially permeable to allow water absorption by osmosis (see page 50).

- As they absorb more water by osmosis, the cell sap becomes more dilute compared with neighbouring cells. Water therefore moves to these adjacent cells which become more diluted themselves, so osmosis continues across the cortex.

Remember that active transport needs energy, so mitochondria will be close to the carrier molecules on the membranes.

- They have carrier proteins in the cell membranes to allow mineral ions to be absorbed by active transport.

Passage of water into the vascular system

Once absorbed by osmosis, water needs to pass to the xylem vessels in order to move up the plant. First it must move across the cortex of the root and through the endodermis before entering the xylem. The mechanism of passage is not known but there are three theories:

- **apoplast** route, where the water is considered to pass between the cells
- **symplast** route, where the water is considered to pass via the cytoplasm of the cells via **plasmodesmata** (cytoplasmic strands connecting one cell to another)
- **vacuolar** route, where the water is considered to pass through the tonoplast then through the sap vacuole of each cell.

Note the different theories for water transport across the width of the root.

movement of water across the cortex

Casparian strip

Water moves across the cortex and needs to pass through the endodermal cells before entering the xylem vessels of the vascular system. Each cell of the endodermis has a waterproof band around it, just like a ribbon around a box. This means that water must pass through the cell in some way, rather than around the outside. If water moves by the apoplast route up to this point, then it must now move into the symplast or vacuolar pathways.

Casparian strip of the endodermal cells

Once the water has passed through the endodermis and navigated the pericycle then it must pass into the xylem for upward movement to the leaves and to the tissues.

How does water move up the vascular system to the leaves?

Water moves into the xylem vessels in the vascular system in the centre of the root; it enters via bordered pits. The xylem is internally lined with lignin. This substance is waterproof and it also gives great strength to the xylem vessels, which are tube shaped. Much of the strength of a plant comes from cells toughened by lignin. A Giant Redwood tree is many metres high but water is still able to reach all the cells. Water moves up the xylem for the following reasons.

> Remember that the xylem is part of the mass flow system ensuring that all cells receive their requirements.

- Root pressure gives an initial upward force to water in the xylem vessels. This can be shown by cutting off a shoot near soil level. Some sap will pour vertically out of the xylem of the remaining exposed xylem.
- Water moves up the xylem by capillarity which is the upward movement of a fluid in a narrow bore tube – xylem has very narrow vessels.
- Capillarity occurs because the water molecules have an attraction for each other (cohesion) so when one water molecule moves others move with it.
- Capillarity has another component – the fact that the water molecules are attracted to the sides of the vessels pulls the water upwards (adhesion).
- Transpiration causes a very negative water potential in the mesophyll of the leaves. Water in the xylem is of higher water potential and so moves up the xylem.

> The factors in the list are known as the cohesion-tension theory and explain how water moves up the xylem.

Xylem vessels die at the end of their maturation phase. The lignin produced inside the cells finally results in death. The young xylem cells end to end, finally produce a long tube-like structure (vessel) through which water passes. Xylem can still transport water after the death of the plant.

Mineral ions are also transported in the xylem.

How is water lost from a leaf?

AQA ▷ 2.7

Water moves up the xylem and into the mesophyll of a leaf. The process by which water is lost from any region of a plant is transpiration. Water can be lost from areas such as a stem, but most water is lost by evaporation through the stomata. Each stoma is a pore which can be open or closed and is bordered at either side by a guard cell. The diagrams show an open stoma and a closed stoma.

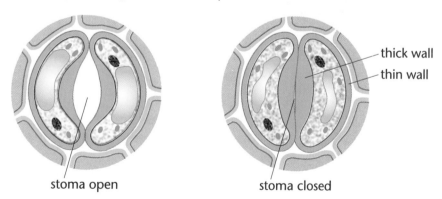

thick wall

thin wall

stoma open   stoma closed

> **KEY POINT**
>
> Transpiration from a leaf takes place as follows:
> - the air spaces in the mesophyll become saturated with water vapour (higher water potential)
> - the air outside the leaf may be of lower humidity (more negative water potential)
> - this causes water molecules to diffuse from the mesophyll of the leaf to the outside.

Some water can escape through the cell junctions and membranes. This is known as cuticular transpiration. In the dark all stomata are closed. Even so, there is still water loss by cuticular transpiration.

How do the guard cells open and close?

In the presence of light:

- K^+ ions are actively transported into the guard cells from adjacent cells
- malate is produced from starch
- K^+ ions and malate accumulate in the guard cells
- this causes an influx of water molecules
- the cell wall of each guard cell is thin in one part and thick in another
- the increase in hydrostatic pressure leads to the opening of the stomata.

Closing of the stomata is the reverse of this process. Under different conditions the stomata can be partially open. The rate of transpiration can increase in warm, dry conditions or decrease at the opposite extreme.

Measuring the rate of transpiration

This is done indirectly by using a potometer. This instrument works on the following principle: for every molecule of water lost by transpiration, one is taken up by the shoot.

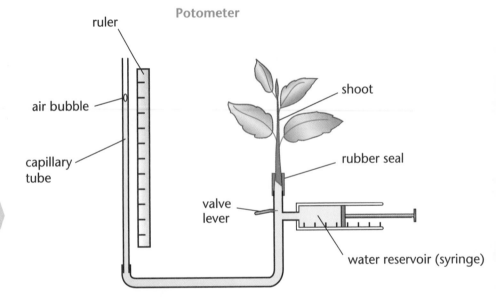

Note that a living shoot may be photosynthesising whilst attached to the instrument. Only a minute amount of water would be used in this process. The instrument gives an accurate measure of transpiration.

The potometer is used as follows:

- a shoot is cut and the end is quickly put in water to prevent an air lock in the xylem
- the potometer is filled under water so that the capillary tube is full
- all air bubbles are removed from the water
- the shoot is put into the rubber seal
- the valve is changed to allow water uptake
- the amount of water taken up by the shoot per unit time is measured
- the shoot can be tested under various conditions.

Xerophytes

AQA 2.7

These are plants which have special adaptations to survive in drying, environmental conditions where many plants would become desiccated and die. The plants survive well because of a combination of the following features:

- thick cuticle to reduce evaporation
- reduced number of stomata
- smaller and fewer leaves to reduce surface area
- hairs on plant to reduce air turbulence
- protected stomata to prevent wind access
- aerodynamic shape to prevent full force of wind
- deep root network to absorb maximum water
- some store of water in modified structures, e.g. the stem of a cactus.

In an exam you may be given a photomicrograph of a xerophytic plant which you have not seen before. Look for *some* of the features covered in the bullet points opposite.

A cactus is a good example of a xerophyte. It makes excellent use of what little water there is available, and holds on to what it does manage to absorb really well. Its cuticle and epidermis are so thick that metabolic water released from the cells during night time respiration is retained for photosynthesis during the day. Nothing is wasted!

Progress check

Water is absorbed into a plant by the root hairs.

(a) The water potential of the root hair cells is more negative than in the soil water. Is this statement true or false?

(b) Describe:

(i) the apoplast route across the cortex

(ii) the symplast route across the cortex.

(a) true

(b) (i) water is considered to pass on the outside of the cell membrane

(ii) water passes through the cytoplasm of the cells through plasmodesmata.

Sample question and model answer

Note that haemoglobin is able to pick up a lot of oxygen, even at low partial pressure.

(a) The graph shows the oxygen dissociation curve for human haemoglobin.

Use the information in the graph to help you answer the following questions.

(i) What is the advantage of haemoglobin as a respiratory pigment when oxygen in the air is at the low partial pressure 6 kPa? [1]

Even at a low partial pressure a lot of oxygen (70%) is taken up by the haemoglobin of a red blood cell.

The fact that haemoglobin is able to carry oxygen is important. However, it is just as important that the oxygen is off-loaded at tissues needing it. This is only possible because carbon dioxide is found at the tissues.

(ii) Explain the effect on the oxygen dissociation curve of a high partial pressure of carbon dioxide at a muscle. [2]

The curve is moved to the right and down so that oxygen is released.

(iii) Fetal haemoglobin has a greater affinity for oxygen than maternal haemoglobin. Draw a curve on the graph to show the oxygen dissociation curve for fetal haemoglobin. [1]

See graph opposite.

(b) The diagram shows **one** stage in the cardiac cycle.

Always look for the valves. If the heart valve is open then the chamber behind it is contracting.

(i) Which stage of the cardiac cycle is shown in the diagram? Give **two** reasons for your answer. [3]

atrial systole
the atrioventricular valves are open/blood flows through the atrioventricular valves,
semi-lunar valves are closed.

(ii) Write an X in one chamber to show the position of the atrioventricular node (AVN). [1]

(iii) How does the AVN stimulate the contraction of the ventricles? [1]

Passes electrical impulses to Purkinje tissue/Bundle of His.

Practice examination questions

1   The diagram shows a capillary bed in the upper part of the skin. The arteriole is constricted.

Use the information in the diagram and your own knowledge to answer the questions below.

(a) As a result of arteriole constriction, to where would the blood flow?   [1]

(b) Explain how this would help maintain the body temperature.   [4]

2   The table shows data about a person's heart before and after a training programme.

	Before training	*After training*
heart stroke rate	90 ml	120 ml
heart rate at rest	75 bpm	60 bpm
maximum heart rate	170 bpm	190 bpm

(a) Over a five minute period at rest before training, the cardiac output of the person was 33.75 litres.

How much blood would leave the heart, during the same time, whilst the person was at rest, after training?   [2]

(b) After training, the maximum heart rate increased by 20 bpm. Explain the advantage of this increase to an athlete.   [4]

(c) After training there are other changes in the body.

Explain:

(i) **two** changes which would improve the efficiency of the respiratory system.   [2]

(ii) the effect of training on the muscles.   [2]

Practice examination questions (continued)

3 The diagram shows a freshly cut, leafy shoot attached to a potometer. This was used to measure the amount of water taken up by the shoot under different conditions.

(a) What assumption must be made when using this apparatus to measure the rate of transpiration? [1]

(b) An air-lock can occur in the shoot which prevents water uptake.

   (i) In which plant tissue could an air-lock occur? [1]

   (ii) Describe the practical details by which a student could make sure that there was no air-lock in the shoot. [2]

(c) The radius of the capillary tube of the potometer was 1 mm. When a Sumach leaf was measured the air bubble moved 32 mm in one minute. Calculate the volume of water in mm^3 which would be taken up by the leaf in one hour under the same environmental conditions. [3]

4 *Agave americana* is a xerophytic plant which grows in the deserts of Mexico.

Agave americana

Suggest **three** ways in which the plant is adapted to survive periods of very low rainfall. [3]

5 The diagram shows nerves linking the medulla oblongata with the heart.

(a) Name part X. [1]

(b) What effect do the following have on the heart:

   (i) vagus nerve

   (ii) sympathetic nerve

   (iii) adrenaline? [3]

Chapter 6

Genes and cell division

The following topics are covered in this chapter:

- *DNA and the genetic code*
- *Cell division*

6.1 DNA and the genetic code

After studying this section you should be able to:

- *recall the structure of DNA*
- *outline the role of DNA in the synthesis of protein*
- *use organic base codes of DNA to identify amino acid sequences*

LEARNING SUMMARY

Deoxyribonucleic acid (DNA) and chromosome structure

AQA ▶ 2.2, 2.3

Each chromosome in a nucleus consists of a series of genes. A gene is a section of a chemical called DNA and each gene controls the production of a polypeptide important to the life of an organism. Deoxyribonucleic acid (DNA) is made up of a number of nucleotides joined together in a double helix shape.

> You need to be aware that many nucleotides join together to form the polymer, DNA.

Each nucleotide consists of a phosphate group, a molecule of deoxyribose sugar and an organic base. Phosphate and pentose sugar units link to form the backbone of the DNA. Repeated linking of the monomer nucleotides forms the polynucleotide chains of DNA.

> Each strand of DNA is said to be complementary to the other. **Examination tip:** be ready to identify one strand when given the matching complementary strand.

Each DNA molecule is made up of two polynucleotide chains. The two chains are held together by hydrogen bonds between the bases.

The organic base of each nucleotide can be any one of adenine, thymine, cytosine or guanine. Adenine forms hydrogen bonds with thymine and cytosine with guanine.

The two chains then twist up to form a double helix.

Why does the DNA of one organism differ from the DNA of another?

Differences in the DNA of organisms such as humans and houseflies lie in the different sequences of the organic bases. Each sequence of bases is a code to make a protein, usually vital to the life of an organism.

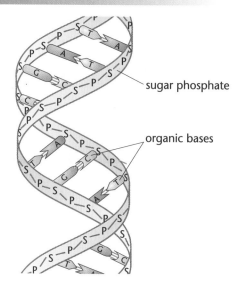

sugar phosphate

organic bases

A single nucleotide

phosphate

pentose sugar — organic base

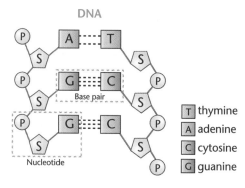

DNA

Base pair

Nucleotide

T	thymine
A	adenine
C	cytosine
G	guanine

How does DNA control protein production?

AQA 22

Each different polypeptide is made of a specific order of amino acids and so DNA must code for this order. The length of DNA that codes for one polypeptide is called a gene.

> **KEY POINT**
>
> Each three adjacent bases code for one amino acid in the polypeptide. The genetic code is therefore a *triplet* code.

The table below shows all the triplet sequences of organic bases found along DNA strands and the coding function of each.

Genetic code functions of DNA

Use the key to identify the amino acids in the table opposite.

Amino acid	Abbreviation
alanine	Ala
arginine	Arg
asparagine	Asn
aspartic acid	Asp
cysteine	Cys
glutamine	Gln
glutamic acid	Glu
glycine	Gly
histidine	His
isoleucine	Iso
leucine	Leu
lysine	Lys
methionine	Met
phenylalanine	Phe
proline	Pro
serine	Ser
threonine	Thr
tryptophan	Trp
tyrosine	Tyr
valine	Val

		Second organic base								Third organic base
		A		*G*		*T*		*C*		
A	A A A	Phe	A G A	Ser	A T A	Tyr	A C A	Cys	A
	A A G		A G G		A T G		A C G		G
	A A T	Leu	A G T		A T T	stop	A C T	stop	T
	A A C		A G C		A T C	stop	A C C	Trp	C
G	G A A		G G A		G T A	His	G C A		A
	G A G	Leu	G G G	Pro	G T G		G C G	Arg	G
	G A T		G G T		G T T	Gln	G C T		T
	G A C		G G C		G T C		G C C		C
T	T A A		T G A		T T A	Asn	T C A	Ser	A
	T A G	Ile	T G G	Thr	T T G		T C G		G
	T A T		T G T		T T T	Lys	T C T	Arg	T
	T A C	Met	T G C		T T C		T C C		C
C	C A A		C G A		CTA	Asp	C C A		A
	C A G	Val	C G G	Ala	CTG		C C G	Gly	G
	C A T		C G T		CTT	Glu	C CT		T
	C A C		C G C		CTC		C C C		C

Each triplet code is *non-overlapping*. This means that each triplet of three bases is a code, then the next three, and so on along the DNA.

- AAA codes for the amino acid phenylalanine
- GAG codes for the amino acid leucine
- GAC codes for the amino acid leucine

There are more triplet codes than there are amino acids. This is known as the *degenerate code*, because an amino acid such as leucine can be coded for by up to six different codes. Some triplets do not code for amino acids but mark the beginning or end of polypeptides. They are *stop or start* triplets.

Introns

In 1977, it was discovered that many genes in eukaryotic organisms were 'split genes'. Mixed in with the DNA that codes for the protein are lengths of DNA that do not code for anything. These lengths are called *introns*. There are also areas of bases between genes that do not seem to code for any proteins.

Some of these non-coding lengths of DNA have unique repeat patterns that are used in genetic finger-printing.

6.2 Cell division

How do cells prepare for division?

AQA   2.5

Before cells divide they must first make an exact copy of their DNA by using a supply of organic bases, pentose sugar molecules and phosphates. The method by which DNA is copied is called semi-conservative replication. The diagram (right) shows this taking place.

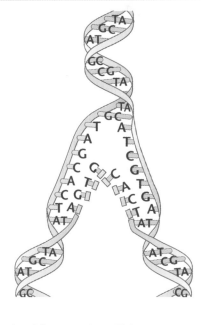

> Remember that as the DNA unwinds each single strand is a **complement** to the other. This means that each has the **matching** series of organic bases.

● The DNA begins to unwind under the influence of the enzyme DNA helicase.
● Hydrogen bonds between the two chains then break and the two strands separate.
● Each complementary strand then acts as a template to build its opposite strand from free nucleotides.
● The enzyme DNA polymerase joins the nucleotides together. This process results in the production of two identical copies of double-stranded DNA.

Evidence for the semi-conservative replication of DNA

Exam questions are often based on experimental data. Apply your knowledge of principles learned during the course and this will be helpful.

The first real evidence came from the results of an experiment carried out by two researchers, Meselson and Stahl.

Bacteria were cultured with a heavy isotope of nitrogen located in the organic bases of their DNA.

The bacteria were then supplied with bases containing the normal light nitrogen atoms. They replicated their DNA using these bases. Their population increased.

Each molecule of DNA of the next generation had one strand containing heavy nitrogen and one strand containing light nitrogen. The mass of the DNA was therefore midway between the original heavy form and normal light DNA.

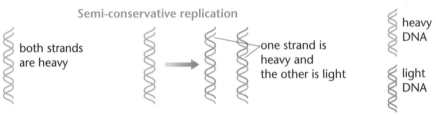

Semi-conservative replication

both strands are heavy

one strand is heavy and the other is light

heavy DNA

light DNA

Make sure that you can predict what would happen if the bacteria replicated again.

Semi-conservative therefore means that as DNA splits into its two single strands, each of the new strands is made of newly acquired bases. The other strand, part of the original DNA, remains.

Types of cell division

AQA 2.5

Cells divide for the purposes of growth, repair and reproduction. Not all cells can divide but there are two ways in which division may occur: mitosis and meiosis.

In most organisms, the chromosomes in each cell can be arranged in pairs. Each cell therefore has two copies of each gene.

When the chromosomes are in pairs, the cell is said to be diploid and the pairs are called homologous pairs.

Be careful of the spelling of mitosis and meiosis; examiners may penalise you if they are spelt incorrectly.

Mitosis produces genetically identical copies of cells with the same number of chromosomes for growth and repair.

Meiosis produces cells that have half the number of chromosomes, one from each pair. These cells are haploid and are used as gametes.

Meiosis introduces variation because the pairs of chromosomes can be split up in many different ways. This is called independent assortment.

Genetic material can also be exchanged between homologous chromosomes. This is called crossing over.

The cell cycle and mitosis

AQA 2.5

The length of time between a cell being formed and it dividing is called the cell cycle. This can be divided up into a number of different phases:

- G1 phase – the cell grows making new proteins and more organelles
- S phase – the DNA of the chromosomes is replicated by semi-conservative replication
- G2 – more organelles are made and a spindle forms
- M phase – this is mitosis involving the separating of the genetic material into two nuclei
- C phase – cytokinesis, where the cell divides into two.

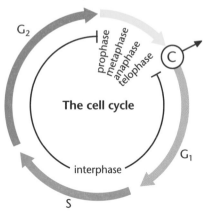

The cell cycle

Remember that DNA replication takes place before cell division in **interphase** (see page 76). This is not an integral phase of mitosis or meiosis.

The length of the cell cycle varies between different types of cells. Some cells never divide once formed but cells of the bone marrow divide about every eight hours. Interphase usually takes up 95% or more of the whole cell cycle.

Be ready to analyse photomicrographs of all phases of mitosis. If you can spot 10 pairs of chromosomes at the end of telophase, then this is the original diploid number of the parent cell.

Interphase is the period of time between cell divisions. It is made up of G1, S and G2 phases. Once cells start mitosis, they all go through a similar sequence of events. This is shown in the diagrams.

1 Prophase

Each chromosome forms two chromatids joined by a centromere. Two centrioles begin to move forming a spindle.

— chromatid

— centriole

2 Metaphase

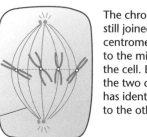

The chromatids, still joined by a centromere move to the middle of the cell. Each of the two chromatids has identical DNA to the other.

spindle —

3 Anaphase

The spindle fibres join to the centromeres. The spindle fibres shorten and the centromeres split. The separated chromatids are now chromosomes.

4 Telophase

Identical chromosomes move to each pole. The nuclear membrane re-forms. The cell membrane narrows at the middle and two daughter cells are formed.

Practice examination questions

1   The diagram below shows a stage in the process of mitosis.

(a) Give the stage of mitosis shown.   [1]

(b) How many chromosomes would there be in the daughter cells?   [2]

2   The table below shows the relative organic base proportions found in human, sheep, salmon and wheat DNA.

	Proportion of organic bases in DNA (%)			
Organism	Adenine	Guanine	Thymine	Cytosine
human	30.9	19.9	29.4	19.8
sheep	29.3	21.4	28.3	21.0
salmon	29.7	20.8	29.1	20.4
wheat	27.3	22.7	27.1	22.8

(a) Refer to the proportion of organic bases in salmon DNA to explain the association between specific bases.   [2]

(b) Suggest a reason for the small difference in proportion of the organic bases adenine and thymine in sheep.   [1]

(c) All species possess adenine, guanine, thymine and cytosine in their DNA. Account for the fact that each species is different.   [2]

Classification and biodiversity

The following topics are covered in this chapter:

- *Classification*
- *Biodiversity*

7.1 Classification

After studying this section you should be able to:

- *understand why and how organisms are classified*
- *describe the binomial system of naming organisms*
- *describe some of the more recent techniques used to classify organisms*

LEARNING SUMMARY

Classifying and naming

AQA ▸ 2.8

It is estimated that there are more than 10 million different kinds of living organisms alive on Earth. The study of the range of different organisms is called systematics. For centuries, scientists have tried to classify organisms into groups and give them names.

> The system of classifying organisms into groups is called taxonomy and the system of naming is called nomenclature.
>
> **KEY POINT**

Organisms are put into groups based on the largest number of common characteristics. Firstly, they are put into one of five large groups called kingdoms.

The table shows the characteristics of organisms in the five kingdoms:

Try this!

Pretty **P**olly **F**inds **P**arrots **A**ttractive.

It will help you to remember the kingdoms!

You may be tested on your knowledge of characteristics across the kingdoms.

Information will usually be given for any subgroup tasks.

The table includes some of the main features of each kingdom.

Prokaryotae and Protoctista tend to give more of a challenge than some of the other kingdoms, and are examined more often.

→ *increase in complexity*				
Prokaryotae	*Protoctista*	*Fungi*	*Plantae*	*Animalia*
very simple cells with few organelles	unicellular cells with membrane-bound organelles	heterotrophic nutrition	multicellular organisms which are photosynthetic	multicellular organisms which are heterotrophic
no membrane-bound organelles	some are photo-synthetic, but many have heterotrophic nutrition	some sapro-trophic, some parasitic	cells have cellulose cell wall, sap vacuole and chloroplasts	no cell walls no sap vacuoles
if there are flagellae, then not 9 + 2 system of microtubules		consists of thread-like hyphae, chitin cell walls		
DNA in strands, no true nucleus	reproduction usually involves fission	many nuclei in hyphae, not in one per cell organisation	reproduce by seeds, or by spores, some sexual, some asexual.	
e.g. bacteria and cyanobacteria	e.g. algae and protozoa	reproduction involves the production of spores		

Each kingdom can be subdivided into a number of progressively smaller groups. Ultimately, this leads to an individual type of organism, a species.

The seven groups can be difficult to remember. Try the easy way!

King Penguins
Climb Over Frozen
Grassy Slopes

The first letter of each word will help you remember. It is a mnemonic which is an excellent strategy to aid recall.

The hierarchy of the groups is shown below.

	Example 1	*Example 2*
Kingdom	Animalia	Animalia
Phylum	Chordata	Arthropoda
Class	Mammalia	Insecta
Order	Primates	Lepidoptera
Family	Hominidae	Pieridae
Genus	Homo	Pieris
Species	sapiens	brassica

What is a species?

The smallest classification group is the species.

Remember, similar organisms such as horses and donkeys can mate to produce mules, but mules are infertile.

> **KEY POINT**
> Organisms are members of the same species if they can breed together to produce fertile offspring.

Naming organisms

Most organisms are known by common names. We use these names all the time. The problem is that an organism may be known by different names or sometimes different organisms can have the same common name. A scientist called Linnaeus introduced a scientific naming system so that each species could have a unique scientific name. This system is called the binomial system.

The name consists of two parts, the name of the genus written with a capital letter and the name of the species, written in lower case.

Notice that binomial names are always typed in italics or underlined if handwritten.

Panthera leo

Panthera tigris

Modern classification techniques

AQA 2.8

For centuries, organisms were classified according to observable physical features. This might be the structure of an animal's skull or the shape of a plant's leaves. Scientists can now use a range of different techniques.

* Microscopic structure – modern electron microscopes have shown that bacteria and other single-celled organisms such as amoeba have completely different cell structure and so they are now put into different kingdoms: *Prokaryotae* and *Protoctista*.

- Genetic differences – it is now possible to compare the DNA base sequences of different organisms. This can be done by a process called DNA hybridisation. Short, single-stranded sections of DNA are produced from one species and the extent to which they bind with DNA from another species is measured.
- Biochemical differences – the occurrence of different biochemical molecules is often a good indicator of relationships. It is also possible to work out and compare the amino acid sequence of common proteins.
- Immunological evidence – antibodies against human proteins can be made and then tested against proteins from other animals. The more effective the antibodies are, then the closer the evolutionary relationship is between humans and the other animal.

> Immunological results give the following % similarities to man:
> chimpanzee 97%,
> gibbon 92%,
> lemur 37%,
> pig 8%

The aim of modern classification systems is to use a range of techniques to produce a system that classifies organisms based on their evolutionary relationships.

> **KEY POINT**
>
> A system based on evolutionary relationships is called a phylogenetic system.

7.2 Biodiversity

> **LEARNING SUMMARY**
>
> After studying this section you should be able to:
>
> - *understand what is meant by the term biodiversity*
> - *explain why there is so much biodiversity on Earth*

What is biodiversity?

AQA   2.11

Biodiversity is a measure of the variation between different living organisms. It could be:

- genetic diversity – the differences between the genes in a species
- species diversity – the number of different species in a community
- ecosystem or habitat diversity – the variety of different areas where organisms can live.

A few definitions

A habitat: an area in which an organism lives.

A population: all the organisms of one species living in a habitat.

A community: all the different species (different populations) living in a habitat.

An ecosystem: all the living organisms (biotic) and inorganic parts (abiotic) of a habitat.

A niche is where an organism lives and its role in that ecosystem.

> A pond is a habitat containing populations such as stickleback and pondweed. All the organisms make up the community and the organisms, the water, the mud, etc. are an ecosystem.

Estimating populations

Often a full count of organisms in an ecosystem is not possible because of the size of the ecosystem. A sampling technique is used which requires a quadrat. This is a small area enclosed by wire or wood, around 0.25 m^2. When placed in the ecosystem the organisms inside the area can be counted, as well as the abiotic factors which influence their distribution. Ecologists use units to measure organisms within the quadrats. Frequency (f) is an indication of the presence of an organism in a quadrat area. This gives no measure of numbers. However the usual unit is that of density, the numbers of the organism per unit area. Sometimes percentage cover is used, an indication of how much of the quadrat area is occupied.

Point quadrat

string or wire

count organisms only at the intersections

Consider a survey of two species *Taraxacum officinale* (dandelion) and *Plantago major* (Great plantain) of the lawn habitat shown below.

A simplified results table

Quadrat no.	Dandelion
1	2
2	12
3	15
4	3
5	4
6	8
7	7
8	10
9	9
10	15

mean = 8.5 per quadrat

$Dm^{-2} = 34$

Lawn habitat

dandelion

great plantain

It is important to use a suitable technique when surveying with quadrats. When you observe a habitat which appears homogeneous or uniform, like a field yellow with buttercups, then you should use random quadrat placement. The area should be gridded, numbers given to each sector of the grid, then a random number generator used. The probability of the numbers in one quadrat representing a field would be very low. In practice the mean numbers from large numbers of quadrats do represent the true numbers in a habitat.

The index of biodiversity

This is used as a measure of the range and numbers of species in an area.

$$\text{index } d = \frac{N(N-1)}{\Sigma\, n(n-1)}$$

N = total no. of all individuals of all species in the area
n = total no. of individuals of one species in an area
Σ = the sum of

Consider this example of animals in a small pond

In another pond there were:

crested newt	45
stickleback	4
leech	18
great pond snail	10

d = 2.6

Look at both indices. 6.05 is an indicator of greater diversity. The higher number indicates greater diversity.

crested newt	8
stickleback	20
leech	15
great pond snail	20
dragonfly larva	2
stonefly larva	10
water boatman	6
caddisfly larva	30
N =	111

$$d = \frac{111 \times 110}{(8 \times 7) + (20 \times 19) + (15 \times 14) + (20 \times 19) + (2 \times 1) + (10 \times 9) + (6 \times 5) + (30 \times 29)}$$

$$d = \frac{12\,210}{2018} \quad \text{so} \quad d = 6.05$$

Sources of biodiversity

AQA 2.1

What is variation?

Species throughout the biosphere differ from each other.

Variation describes the differences which exist in organisms throughout the biosphere. This variation consists of differences between species as well as differences within the same species. An organism's characteristics (phenotype) is a combination of the action of an organism's genes (genotype) and the influence of the environment.

genotype + environment = phenotype

Therefore variation can depend on environmental factors and genetic diversity. The variation that is produced can be either continuous or discontinuous.

Continuous variation

This is shown when there is a range of small incremental differences in a feature of organisms in a population. An example of this is height in humans. If the height of each pupil in a school is measured then from the shortest pupil to the tallest, there are very small differences across the distribution. This is shown by the graph below which shows smooth changes in height across a population. This type of variation is shown when features are controlled by polygenic inheritance. A number of genes interact to produce the expressed feature.

Remember that a species shows continuous variation when there are small incremental differences, e.g. height of people in a town. Beginning with the smallest and ending with the tallest there would probably be at least one person at each height, at 1cm increments. A smooth gradation of differences!

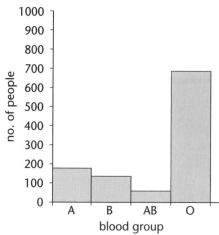

Discontinuous variation

This is shown when a characteristic is expressed in discrete categories. Humans have four discrete blood groups, A, B, AB or O. There are no intermediates, the differences are clear cut!

Mean and standard deviation

The variation shown by most populations can be described graphically. The variable usually forms a bell-shaped curve called a normal distribution.

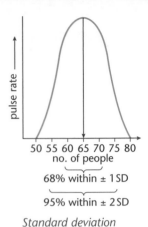

Standard deviation

The **mean** is the value at the peak of the curve. The **standard deviation** describes how the values are spread out. The higher the standard deviation, then the more variation there is.

> In a normal distribution, 68% of the values are within one standard deviation either side of the mean and 95% are within two.

The influence of the environment

The many different habitats on Earth provide different conditions for organisms to live in. There may be variations in a number of different factors that can affect organisms:

- **climatic** factors, e.g. temperature, water availability, light
- **edaphic** (soil) factors, e.g. pH, minerals and oxygen content
- **biotic** factors, e.g. competition.

Genetic diversity

Although organisms of the same species have the same genes, they show genetic variation because they have different alleles. These alleles are produced by **mutation**.

Sometimes genetic variation is reduced because factors can limit the variety of alleles. Some of these factors are manmade and others are naturally occurring.

Selective breeding

Mankind has used selective breeding to produce many of the plants and animals that we rely on for food. Organisms that have the desired characteristics are allowed to breed, others are prevented from breeding. Over many generations, the population changes and shows the characteristics that are wanted. This also has the effect of limiting the variation of alleles in the population and therefore the genetic diversity.

The founder effect

The founder effect happens when a new population is formed by a small number of individuals. It might be a few birds landing on a newly formed island. The individuals will not have a great variety of alleles and so the population that they form will be restricted.

Genetic bottlenecks

A population may decrease in number due to natural events or man's influence. If the numbers become very small then the number of alleles will be limited. If the population recovers then the genetic diversity will be limited.

> The numbers of Hawaiian goose dropped to about 30 birds in 1950 due to a number of factors such as over-hunting. Their numbers are starting to recover but their genetic diversity is really low.

Genetic variation in bacteria

Bacteria can reproduce every 20 minutes in ideal conditions.

Natural selection usually takes many thousands of years to produce changes, but in bacterial populations, changes can occur more rapidly. This is because they reproduce so quickly.

Mutations can occur to the DNA of bacteria when the DNA is copied prior to cell division. These mutations are passed on to the new bacteria and this is called vertical gene transmission. The new alleles may give the bacteria a selective advantage.

Although bacteria do not reproduce sexually, they can transfer DNA from one bacterium to another. This is called conjugation. It happens like this:
- One bacterial cell produces a thin tube from the cell membrane.
- This attaches to another bacterium.
- This allows small rings of DNA called plasmids to be transferred.

The passing on of genes by conjugation is called horizontal gene transmission.

Antibiotic resistance

One example of the importance of genetic variation in bacteria is their resistance to antibiotics.

> Antibiotics are substances produced by living organisms that destroy microorganisms or inhibit their growth.
>
> **KEY POINT**

Antibiotics prevent bacteria from making the cell wall properly. This means that when the bacteria take up water by osmosis the cell wall is too weak and bursts. The bacteria then die. This is called osmotic lysis.

Random mutations have occurred that allow bacteria to be resistant to the action of antibiotics like penicillin. These bacteria are more likely to survive and pass on the resistance by vertical gene transmission. This has produced strains that are resistant to certain antibiotics.

More worryingly, the genes can be passed from one strain to another by horizontal gene transmission. This has produced strains of bacteria such as MRSA and TB bacteria that are resistant to many different antibiotics.

Sample question and model answer

The quagga is an extinct mammal that looked like a zebra but had stripes only on its head, neck and forebody. The quagga lived in Africa until the last animal was shot in the late 1870s. The last specimen died in 1883 in a zoo.

The quagga, named *Equus quagga*, was originally thought to be a separate species to the plains Zebra.

Over the last fifty years or so, the markings of many individual zebras have been recorded by scientists.

Because of the great variation in stripe patterns, taxonomists were left with a problem. Was the quagga a separate species or was it a type of zebra? The quagga was the first extinct creature to have its DNA studied. Recent research using DNA from preserved specimens has demonstrated that the quagga was not a separate species at all, but a variety of the plains zebra, *Equus burchelli*.

Questions about natural selection always have similar mark schemes. Just make sure that you apply this mark scheme to the particular situation.

(a) What is the name of the genus that both the plains zebra and the quagga belong to? [1]

Equus

(b) What type of variation does the stripe pattern in zebras demonstrate? [1]

Continuous variation

(c) How could scientists use the DNA to investigate the relationship between the zebra and the quagga? [2]

Use DNA hybridisation.
The DNA is split into single strands and then scientists see how well it binds with zebra DNA strands.

(d) The plains zebra may have more stripes than the quagga because the stripes provide better camouflage on the plains.
How might this pattern have developed by natural selection? [3]

Zebras show variation and are born with different patterns of stripes.
More stripes make the zebra better camouflaged and so more likely to survive.
These zebras survive, breed and pass on the genes for more stripes.

Practice examination questions

1 The following key distinguishes between the five kingdoms.

1	Organisms without membrane bound organelles	A
	Organisms with membrane bound organelles	GO TO 2
2	Organisms have hyphae	B
	Organisms do not have hyphae	GO TO 3
3	Organisms unicellular or colonial	C
	Organisms not unicellular or colonial	GO TO 4
4	Organisms multicellular and have thylakoid membranes in some cells	D
	Organisms multicellular and have no thylakoid membranes in any cells	E

Name kingdoms A, B, C, D and E [5]

2 (a) The song-thrush (*Turdus ericetorum*) and mistle-thrush (*Turdus viscivorus*) are in the same family, *Turdidae*. Large sections of their DNA are common to both species. Complete the table to classify both organisms. [3]

	Mistle-thrush	Song-thrush
Kingdom		
Phylum	Chordata	Chordata
	Aves	
	Passeriformes	Passeriformes
Genus		
Species		

[1]　　　　[1]　　　　[1]

(b) How is it possible to find out if two female animals are from the same species? [1]

3 Students wished to investigate whether a pond in a field was being affected by a nearby cattle feeding station.

They sampled the water in the pond using a net and caught the following organisms:

(a) Use the student' results to produce an index of diversity for the sample. [2]

(b) The students sampled another pond in the same way.
This pond was further from the feeding station and their results produced an index of diversity of 6.90.
What conclusions can be drawn from the students' results? [2]

Human health and disease

The following topics are covered in this chapter:

- *Health and lifestyle*
- *Disease*
- *Immunity*
- *Assisting immunity*

8.1 Health and lifestyle

After studying this section you should be able to:

- *define health*
- *understand how coronary heart disease can be affected by lifestyle*
- *describe the specific effects of smoking tobacco*

LEARNING SUMMARY

How can we achieve good health?

AQA A 1.1

Good health is not just an absence of disease or infirmity. It is the physical, mental and social well-being of a person. The development of a healthy person begins in the uterus. It is important that the mother supplies the fetus with suitable nutrients for development, e.g. amino acids for proteins essential for healthy growth. The mother's diet is important for both her and the fetus.

Following birth, the emotional and social development are equally as important as physical development.

If a person is healthy then they may expect the following:

- an absence of disease
- an absence of pain
- to be fit and have good muscle tone
- an absence of stress
- to get along with other people in society
- to have a long life expectancy.

Coronary heart disease and lifestyle

AQA 1.5

Atherosclerosis is a major health problem caused by eating saturated fats. This circulatory disease may develop as follows:

- yellow fatty streaks develop under the lining of the endothelium on the inside of an artery
- the streaks develop into a fatty lump called an atheroma
- the atheroma is made from cholesterol (taken up in the diet as well as being made in the liver)
- dense fibrous tissue develops as the atheroma grows
- the endothelial lining can split, allowing blood to contact the fibrous atheroma
- the damage may lead to a blood clot and an artery can be blocked.

collagen fibres

endothelium
a healthy artery

atheroma
fat and fibres

clot atheroma so big that
blockage taking place

Remember that the clotting of blood can occur for other reasons. There may be damage at other positions around the body. Blockage of this type is **thrombosis**.

Increasing constriction of an artery caused by atherosclerosis and blood clots reduces blood flow and increases blood pressure. If the artery wall is considerably weakened then a bulge in the side appears, just like a weakened inner tube on a cycle tyre. There is a danger of bursting and the structure is known as an aneurysm.

It is possible for a blood clot formed at an atheroma to break away from its original position. It may completely block a smaller vessel, this is known as an embolism.

Coronary heart disease

If the artery which supplies the heart (coronary artery) is partially blocked, then there is a reduction in oxygen and nutrient supply to the heart itself. This is called coronary heart disease (CHD). The first sign is often angina, the main symptom being sharp chest pains. If total blockage occurs then myocardial infarction (heart attack) takes place.

Lifestyle and CHD

Many aspects of lifestyle influence the condition of the cardiovascular system. CHD is a multi-factorial disease and the risk of developing CHD depends on a number of factors.

Statistically people have a greater chance of avoiding CHD if they:

* consume a low amount of saturated fat in their diet
* do not drink alcohol excessively
* consume a low amount of salt
* do not smoke
* are not stressed most of the time
* exercise regularly.

New drugs called statins are being prescribed in an effort to reduce CHD. They are thought to work by decreasing LDL levels in the blood.

Saturated fats (see lipid structure pages 19–20) are found in large quantities in animal tissues. Eating large quantities of saturated fats seems to increase the risk of CHD. It seems that saturated fat increases the levels of low-density lipoproteins (LDLs) in the blood. LDLs transport cholesterol in the blood and high levels of LDLs seem to increase the risk of atheroma formation. Other fats such as polyunsaturated fats seem to increase the levels of high-density lipoproteins (HDLs). This seems to give some protection against CHD.

Exercise has a protective effect on the heart and circulation. Activities such as jogging, walking, swimming and cycling can:

* reduce the resting heart rate
* increase the strength of contraction of the heart muscle
* increase the stroke volume of the heart (the volume of blood which is propelled during the contractions of the ventricles).

High salt levels have been shown to increase blood pressure, therefore increasing the risk of damage to atheromas.

Smoking also increases blood pressure and makes the blood more likely to clot.

Progress check

(a) Name a specific substance in food which can result in atherosclerosis.
(b) Describe and explain the structural changes which take place in a blood vessel as atherosclerosis develops.
(c) How can the damage caused by an atheroma result in a heart attack?

(a) saturated fat
(b) yellow fatty streaks develop under the cells lining the inside of a blood vessel, the streaks develop into a lump known as an atheroma, the atheroma is made of cholesterol, dense fibrous tissue develops and the lining of the vessel can split.
(c) a blood clot forms which can block the blood vessel completely. Prevention of oxygen supply to the heart results in myocardial infarction (heart attack).

What are the dangers of smoking tobacco?

AQA 1.4

Each person has another choice to make, to smoke or not to smoke. The government health warning on every cigarette packet informs of health dangers but many young people go ahead and ignore the information.

Effects of tobacco smoking

- Nicotine is the active component in tobacco which addicts people to the habit.

- Tars coat the alveoli which slows down exchange of carbon dioxide and oxygen. If less oxygen is absorbed then the smokers will be less active than their true potential.

- Cilia lining bronchial tubes are coated then destroyed, reducing the efficiency in getting rid of pollutants which enter the lungs. These pollutants include the cigarette chemicals themselves.

- Carbon monoxide from the cigarette gases combines with haemoglobin of red blood cells rather than oxygen. This reduces oxygen transport and the smokers become less active than their potential. Ultimately it may lead to heart disease.

- The bronchi and bronchioles become inflamed, a condition known as bronchitis. This causes irritating fluid in the lungs, coughing and increased risk of heart disease. A number of bronchitis sufferers die each year.

- The walls of the alveoli break down reducing the surface area for gaseous exchange. Less oxygen can be absorbed by the lungs, leaving the emphysema sufferers extremely breathless. They increase their breathing rate to compensate but still cannot take in enough oxygen for a healthy life. Chronic emphysema sufferers need an oxygen cylinder to prolong their life.

- Blood vessel elasticity is reduced so that serious damage may occur. Ultimately a heart attack can follow.

- The carcinogens (cancer-causing chemicals) of the tobacco can result in lung cancer. Malignant growths in the lungs develop uncontrollably and cancers may spread to other parts of the body. Death often follows. Smokers have a greater risk of developing other cancers than non-smokers, e.g. more smokers develop cervical cancer.

> Learn the characteristics of each disease carefully. There are so many consequences of smoking that you may well mix them up.

Even non-smokers can develop any of the above symptoms, but the probability of developing them is increased by smoking. Being in a smoky atmosphere each day also increases the chances.

The role of statistics

The government health warning on cigarette packets informs people of the risks of smoking. The WHO (World Health Organisation), governments and local authorities have collected statistics on many diseases over the years. These are used in education packs and posters to warn of risk factors. People can take precautions and use the information to avoid health dangers and take advantage of vaccination programmes.

Where education is not successful then related diseases follow. This acts as a drain on the National Health Service. Many operations which would have been unnecessary are performed to save people's lives, e.g. where coronary blood vessels are dangerously diseased a by-pass operation is the answer. The ideal situation is that education is successful, but realistically the aim is to balance prevention and cure.

8.2 Disease

After studying this section you should be able to:

- *define disease*
- *understand how infectious diseases are transmitted*

LEARNING SUMMARY

What is a disease?

AQA 1.1

A disease is a disorder of a tissue, organ or system of an organism. As a result of a disorder, symptoms are evident. Such symptoms could be the failure to produce a particular digestive enzyme, or a growth of cells in the wrong place. Normal bodily processes may be disrupted, e.g. efficient oxygen transport is impeded by the malarial parasite, *Plasmodium*.

Different types of disease

Infectious disease by pathogens
Pathogens attack an organism and can be passed from one person to another. Many pathogens are spread by a vector which carries them from one organism to another without being affected itself by the disease. Pathogens include bacteria, viruses, protozoa, fungi, parasites and worms.

Genetic diseases
These can be passed from parent to offspring, e.g. haemophilia and cystic fibrosis.

Dietary related diseases
These are caused by the foods that we eat. Too much or too little food may cause disorders, e.g. obesity or anorexia nervosa. Lack of vitamin D causes the bone disease rickets, the symptoms of which are soft weak bones which bend under the body weight.

Environmentally related diseases
Some aspects of the environment disrupt bodily processes, e.g. as a result of nuclear radiation leakage, cancer may develop.

Auto-immune disease
The body in some way attacks its own cells so that processes fail to function effectively.

> Most exam candidates recall that pathogens are responsible for disease. However, there are more causes of disease! If a question asks for different types of disease then giving a range of pathogens will not score many marks. Give genetic diseases, etc.

> An **auto-immune disease** may be **environmentally** caused, e.g. the form of leukaemia where phagocytes destroy a person's red blood cells may be caused by radiation leakage.

How are infectious diseases transmitted?

The pathogens which cause infectious diseases are transmitted in a range of ways.

- Direct contact – sexual intercourse enables the transmission of syphilis bacteria; a person's foot which touches a damp floor at the swimming baths can transfer the Athlete's foot fungus.
- Droplet infection – a sneeze propels tiny droplets of nasal mucus carrying viruses such as those causing influenza.
- Via a vector – if a person with typhoid bacteria in the gut handles food the bacteria can be passed to a susceptible person.
- Via food or water – chicken meat kept in warm conditions encourages the reproduction of *Salmonella* bacteria which are transferred to the human consumer, who has food poisoning as a result.
- Via blood transfusion – as a result of receiving infected blood a person can contract AIDS.

> Be prepared to answer questions about diseases not on your syllabus. The examiners will give data and other information which you will need to interpret. Use your knowledge of the principles of disease transmission, infection, symptoms and cure.

Some infectious diseases have serious consequences to human life. The incidence of infectious diseases may vary according to the climate of the country, the presence of vectors, the social behaviour of people and other factors.

Disease file – cholera

AQA 1.3

Cause of disease

Vibrio cholerae (bacteria) in the faeces or vomit of a human sufferer or human carrier which contaminate water supplies.

Transmission of microorganism

Contaminated water spreads the bacteria. Poor sanitary behaviour of people who are carriers and those who have contracted the disease are responsible. Faeces enters rivers which may be used for bathing, drinking, or irrigation. The bacteria survive outside the human body for around 24 hours. They can also contaminate vegetables and can be passed to a person in this way.

Outline of the course of the disease and symptoms

The bacteria reach the intestines where they breed. They secrete a toxin which increases secretion of chloride ions into the intestine, giving severe diarrhoea. Death is a regular consequence, due to dehydration, but some people do recover.

Prevention

Education about cleanliness and sewage treatment. Good sanitation is vital. Suitable treatment of water to be consumed by people, e.g. chlorination which kills the bacteria. Use of disinfectant also kills the bacteria. Early identification of an outbreak followed by control.

Cure

Tetracycline antibiotics kill organisms in the bowel. Immunisation is not very effective. It will help some individuals but not stop them from being carriers, so epidemics are still likely.

Oral rehydration therapy is usually used to combat the dehydration caused by diarrhoea and vomiting.

Simply drinking water is ineffective because the electrolyte losses also need replacing. The standard treatment is to restore fluids intravenously with water and salts. This requires trained personnel and materials which are not always available.

However, it was discovered that the body can absorb a simple solution containing both sugar and salt. The dry ingredients can be mixed and packaged, and then the solution can be given by people with minimal training. In cholera, the toxin interferes with one transport system in the intestine lining but the sodium-glucose co-transporter still operates. This allows absorption of glucose, sodium and water.

Oral rehydration can therefore be accomplished by drinking frequent small amounts of an oral rehydration solutions.

Disease file – tuberculosis

AQA 1.4

Cause of disease

Mycobacterium tuberculosis (bacterium) via droplet infection.

Transmission of microorganism

Coughs and sneezes of sufferers spread tiny droplets of moisture containing the pathogenic bacteria. People then inhale these droplets and may contract the disease.

Outline of the course of the disease and symptoms

The initial attack takes place in the lungs. The alveoli surfaces and capillaries are vulnerable and lesions occur. Some epithelial tissues begin to grow in number but these cannot carry out gaseous exchange. Inflammation occurs which stimulates painful coughing. Intense coughing takes place which can cause bleeding. There is much weight loss. Weak groups of people, like the elderly, or those underweight are more prone to the disease.

Prevention

Mycobacterium bovis causes tuberculosis in cattle. It can be passed to humans via milk. It causes an intestinal complaint in humans. It is important that cows are kept free of *M. bovis* by antibiotics.

The BCG vaccination is the injection of a weakened form of this microbe. This vaccination stimulates antibodies which are effective against both *M. tuberculosis* and *M. bovis*.

Mass screening using **X-rays** can identify 'shadows' in those people with scar tissue in the lungs.

Sputum testing identifies the presence of the bacteria in sufferers. Sufferers can be treated with antibiotics. Once cured they cannot pass on the pathogen so an epidemic may be prevented.

Skin testing is used. Antigens from dead *Mycobacteria* are injected just beneath the skin. If a person has been previously exposed to the organism then the skin swells which shows that they already have resistance, i.e. they have antibodies already. Anyone whose skin does not swell up is given the **BCG vaccination**. This contains attenuated *Mycobacterium bovis* to stimulate the production of antibodies against both *M. bovis* and *M. tuberculosis*.

Cure

Use of antibiotics such as streptomycin.

8.3 Immunity

After studying this section you should be able to:

- *describe and explain the action of the body's immune system*

LEARNING SUMMARY

The roles of the white blood cells (leucocytes)

AQA ▶ 1.6

There are a number of different types of leucocytes. Most are produced from stem cells in the bone marrow. Different stem cells follow alternative maturation procedures to produce a range of leucocytes. Leucocytes have the ability to recognise self chemicals and non-self chemicals. Only where non-self chemicals are recognised will a leucocyte respond. Proteins and polysaccharides are typical of the complex molecules which can trigger an immune response.

Phagocytes

Phagocytes can move to a site of infection through capillaries, tissue fluid and lymph as well as being found in the plasma. They move towards pathogens which they destroy by the process of phagocytosis. This is often called engulfment and involves the surrounding of a pathogen by pseudopodia to form a food vacuole. Hydrolytic enzymes from lysosomes complete the destruction of the pathogen.

Neutrophils are one type of phagocyte. Proteins in plasma called **opsonins** attach to a pathogen. These opsonins enable the phagocyte to engulf the pathogen.

Macrophages are another type of phagocyte which work alongside T-lymphocytes.

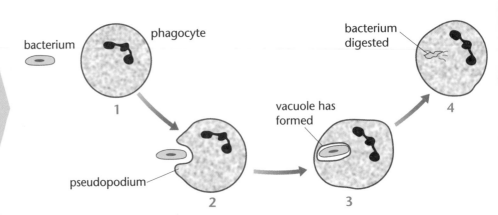

What is an antigen?

AQA A ▶ 1.6

As an individual grows and develops, complex substances such as proteins and polysaccharides are used to form cellular structures. Leucocytes identify these substances in the body as 'self' substances. They are ignored as the leucocytes encounter them daily. 'Non-self substances', e.g. foreign proteins which enter the body, are immediately identified as 'non-self'. These are known as antigens and trigger an immune response.

Lymphocytes

White blood cells (leucocytes) constantly check out proteins around the body. Foreign protein is identified and attack is stimulated.

In addition to phagocytes, there are other leucocytes called lymphocytes. There are two types of lymphocyte, B-lymphocytes and T-lymphocytes.

B-lymphocytes begin development and mature in the bone marrow. They produce antibodies, known as the humoral response.

T-lymphocytes work alongside phagocytes known as macrophages; this is known as the **cell-mediated response**. A macrophage engulfs an antigen. This antigen remains on the surface of the macrophage. T-lymphocytes respond to the antigen, dividing by mitosis to form a range of different types of T-lymphocyte cells.

- **Killer T-lymphocytes** adhere to the pathogen, secrete a toxin and destroy it.
- **Helper T-lymphocytes** stimulate the production of antibodies.
- **Suppressor T-lymphocytes** are inhibitors of the T-lymphocytes and plasma cells. Just weeks after the initial infection, they shut down the immune response when it is no longer needed.
- **Memory T-lymphocytes** respond to an antigen previously experienced. They are able to destroy the same pathogen before symptoms appear.

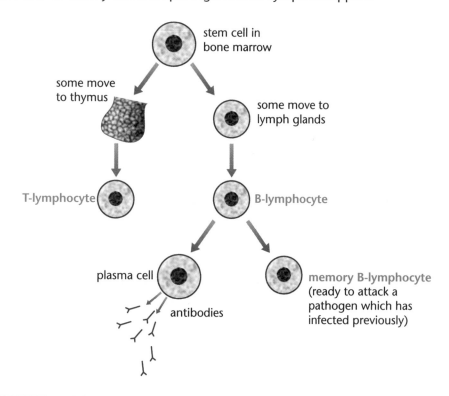

stem cell in bone marrow

some move to thymus

some move to lymph glands

T-lymphocyte

B-lymphocyte

plasma cell

memory B-lymphocyte (ready to attack a pathogen which has infected previously)

antibodies

antigen

bacterium

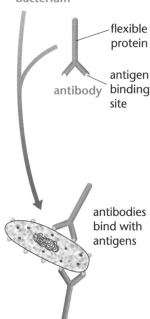

flexible protein

antigen binding site

antibody

antibodies bind with antigens

How do antibodies destroy pathogens?

The diagram on the left shows antibodies binding to antigens. The descriptions below show what can happen immediately after the binding takes place.

There are three main ways in which antibodies destroy pathogens.

- **Precipitation**, by linking many antigens together. This enables the phagocytes to engulf them.
- **Lysis**, where the cell membrane breaks open, killing the cell.
- **Neutralisation** of a chemical released by the pathogen, so that the chemical is no longer toxic.

8.4 Assisting immunity

After studying this section you should be able to:

- describe the origin of different types of immunity
- explain how immunity can be stimulated by vaccinations

LEARNING SUMMARY

Stimulating the immune system

AQA   1.6

Newborn babies are naturally protected against many diseases such as measles and poliomyelitis. This is because they have received antibodies from their mother in two ways:

- across the placenta
- via breast feeding.

This is one major advantage of breast feeding over bottle feeding of babies.

This type of immunity is called passive natural immunity. It is possible to give people injections of antibodies that have been made by another person or animal. This type of immunity is called passive artificial immunity.

> **KEY POINT**
>
> Passive immunity does not last very long. This is because the antibodies do not persist in the blood for very long.

Active immunity

Once a person has recovered from certain diseases, e.g. measles, they rarely contract that disease again. This is because the memory cells formed from B-lymphocytes can survive in the blood for many years. If the antigen reappears, they can rapidly produce a clone of antibody producing cells. This secondary response is rapid and larger than the primary response and the antigen is rapidly destroyed.

This type of immunity is called active natural immunity.

Vaccines consist of dead or weakened (attenuated) forms of pathogens. They stimulate the production of memory cells so that the person develops active artificial immunity.

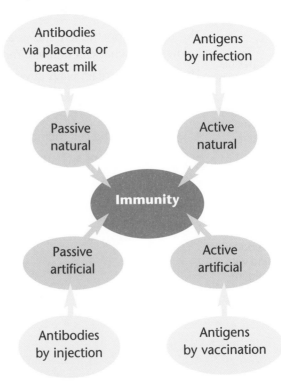

Unfortunately some pathogens show antigenic variation. This change in antigens renders vaccinations ineffective after a while and allows diseases such as influenza to strike many times in slightly different forms.

Scientists are now using antibody producing cells that have been fused with tumour cells. This produces cells that make large quantities of one type of antibody. They are called monoclonal antibodies. Because of their ability to target particular antigens, they might be useful in delivering drugs straight to target cells.

Sample question and model answers

The graph below shows the relative numbers of antibodies in a person's blood after the vaccination of attenuated viruses. Vaccinations were given on day 1 then 200 days later.

In examinations you are regularly given graphs. Make sure that you can link the idea being tested. This should help you recall all of the important concepts needed. All you need to do after this is **apply** your knowledge to the given data.

(a) Why is it important that viruses used in vaccinations are attenuated? [1]

If they were active then the person would contract the disease.

(b) Suggest **two** advantages of giving the second vaccination. [2]

A greater number of antibodies were produced.
The antibodies remain for much longer after the second vaccination.

(c) Which cells produced the antibodies during the primary response? [1]

B-lymphocytes.

(d) Why was there no delay in the secondary response to vaccination? [3]

Because the first vaccination had already been given, memory B-lymphocytes had been produced which respond to the viruses more quickly.

(e) Describe how a virus stimulates the production of antibodies? [3]

Antigen in the protein 'coat' or capsomere stimulate the B-lymphocytes.

If you gave B-lymphocytes as a response it would be wrong! B-lymphocytes secrete antibodies.

(f) Apart from producing antibodies, outline TWO different ways that the body uses to destroy microorganisms. [2]

Phagocytes by engulfment; T-lymphocytes attach to microorganisms and destroy them.

Practice examination questions

1 The illustration shows how the bacterium which causes TB can be transmitted from one person to another.

(a) Name the method of disease transmission shown in the illustration. [1]

(b) Sometimes the bacteria infect people but they do not develop symptoms.

   (i) What term is given to this group of people? [1]

   (ii) Explain why these people may be a greater danger to a community than those who actually suffer from the disease. [2]

2 The diagram shows the response of B-lymphocytes to a specific antigen.

(a) (i) A plasma cell is bigger than a B-lymphocyte.
     Suggest an advantage of this. [1]

   (ii) Describe the precise role of antibodies in the immune response. [3]

   (iii) What is the advantage of memory B-lymphocytes? [2]

(b) What is an auto-immune disease? Give an example. [2]

(c) A person contracts the virus which causes the common cold.
   Suggest why their lymphocytes may fail to destroy the pathogen. [1]

Practice examination answers

Chapter 1 Biological molecules

1 (a) RCOOH   HOCH$_2$
      |
      RCOOH + HOCH
      |
      RCOOH   HOCH$_2$
      fatty acids   glycerol   [2]

   (b) Emulsion test: add the sample to ethanol and mix;
       decant or pour into water;
       if a fat is present a white emulsion forms on the
       surface.   [3]
                                              [Total: 5]

2 (a) peptide bond/peptide link   [1]
   (b) –COOH/carboxylic acid   [1]
   (c) primary structure; amino acids in a chain   [2]
                                              [Total: 4]

Chapter 2 Cells

1 (a) A = phospholipid   B = protein   [2]
   (b) Acts as a channel/pore; to allow molecules in or
       out of the cell.   [1]
   (c) One end is hydrophobic and the other is
       hydrophilic; Hydrophilic tails 'hide' in the centre of
       the membrane;   [2]
                                              [Total: 5]

2 (a) C = Golgi body
       B = Centrioles
       A = Cell membrane
       E = Mitochondria
       D = Rough endoplasmic reticulum   [5]

   (b) Correct measure of width nucleus (~2.0 cm)
       convert to micrometres (20 000 μm)
       divide size by 5 000 (4 μm)   [3]

   (c) Liver cells carry out many functions;
       Need large amounts of energy/ATP   [2]
                                              [Total: 10]

3 (a) cell wall (not cellulose); no true nucleus; no
       mitochondria; plasmids [any two for 2 marks] [2]
   (b) mitochondria; nucleus; Golgi body; large
       ribosomes/rough endoplasmic reticulum
       [any two for 2 marks]   [2]
                                              [Total: 4]

4 (a) lens X = projector; lens Y = objective   [2]
   (b) electrons would collide with air molecules   [1]
   (c) (i) artefact   [1]
       (ii) ignore the artefact, because it is not part of
            normal structure and is only present
            due to preparation of the specimen.   [1]
                                              [Total: 5]

Chapter 3 Enzymes

1 (a) lock and key – the substrate is a similar shape to the active site; it fits in and binds with the active site like a key (substrate) fitting into a lock (active site); induced fit – the substrate is not a matching 'fit' for the active site, but as the substrate approaches, the active site changes into an appropriate shape.

(b) reversible – enters active site but will come out again irreversible – binds permanently with enzymes   [4]
[Total: 4]

2 • The tertiary structure of the enzyme is responsible for the further folding of the protein;
• this gives the shape of the active site;
• the active site in amylase is specific to starch, lipid is unable to bind to the active site of amylase, therefore amylase cannot break down lipid.   [3]
[Total: 3]

3 (a) starch   [1]
(b) thermostable enzymes are effective at high temperatures   [1]
[Total: 2]

4 (a) The substrate molecule collides with the active site of the enzyme; as it approaches, the active site changes shape to become compatible with the substrate shape.   [2]
(b) Non-competitive inhibitor molecule binds with part of enzyme other than the active site; as a result the active site changes shape; so the substrate can no longer bind with the active site.   [3]
[Total: 5]

5 (a) NH_2 (amino group)   [1]

(b) The enzymes then have more ends to attack.   [2]
[Total: 3]

Chapter 4   Exchange

1 (a) (i) No change in size because the water potential inside the cell equals the water potential of the solution outside the cell.   [1]
(ii) The water potential of the solution outside the cell is more negative than the water potential inside the cell.   [1]
(iii) The water potential of the solution outside the cell is less negative than the water potential inside the cell.   [1]

(b) osmosis   [1]
[Total: 4]

2 (a) They both use a protein carrier molecule.   [1]

(b) Active transport needs energy or mitochondria, whereas facilitated diffusion does not.
OR Active transport allows molecules to move from a lower concentrated solution to a higher concentrated solution.
OR Active transport allows molecules to move against a concentration gradient.   [1]
[Total: 2]

3 • a flat, thin blade allows maximum light absorption;
• the leaf has a waxy cuticle to reflect excess light but allow entry of enough light for photosynthesis;
• the mesophyll cells have many chloroplasts to absorb the maximum amount of light;
• the palisade cells pack closely together to absorb the maximum amount of light;

• guard cells open stomata to allow carbon dioxide in and oxygen out during photosynthesis;
• air spaces in the mesophyll store lots of carbon dioxide for photosynthesis;
• xylem of the vascular bundles bring water to the leaf for photosynthesis;
• phloem takes the carbohydrate away from the leaf after photosynthesis.
[any 6 points]   [6]
[Total: 6]

4 (a) alveoli have a very high surface area; they are very close to many capillaries; capillaries are one cell thick/very thin/have squamous epithelia; they are kept damp which facilitates diffusion.   [4]

(b) • there are many gill filaments, which give a very high surface area;
• the gill filaments are very thin;
• they have many capillaries;
• they have gill plates which increase the surface area further;
• the blood and water directions are opposite which maximises diffusion/they use countercurrent flow to maximise diffusion.
[any 4 points]   [4]
[Total: 8]

Chapter 5 Transport

1 (a) to the body core [1]

(b) less blood reaches the superficial capillaries of the skin; so less heat is lost by conduction, convection and radiation; blood in the body core better insulated by the adipose layer of the skin [4]

[Total: 5]

2 (a) 60 x 120 x 5 = 36 000 ml / 36 litres [2]

(b) • blood is transported more quickly;
  • more oxygen taken up at the lungs/more carbon dioxide excreted at the lungs;
  • more oxygen reaches the muscles;
  • more glucose reaches the muscles;
  • so muscles contract more effectively.
  [any 4 points] [4]

(c) (i) • slower breathing rate;
    • more alveoli accessed for exchange;
    • intercostal muscles more effective.
    [any 2 points] [2]

(ii) • improved muscle tone;
    • greater muscular strength;
    • more capillaries in muscles. [any 2 points] [2]

[Total: 10]

3 (a) The amount of water lost by transpiration is exactly matched by the amount taken up by the leaf. [1]

(b) (i) xylem [1]

(ii) fill the potometer under water; operate the valve to get rid of air bubbles; when removing the leaf from the tree, the stalk or petiole must be put in water immediately. [2]

(c) Volume of water = πr^2 x 32 mm x 60

$$= \frac{22}{7} \times 1 \times 1 \times 32 \times 60$$

$$= 6034.3 \text{ mm}^3$$ [3]

[Total: 7]

4 • extensive root system to absorb maximum water;
  • large amount of water storage in leaves;
  • thick cuticle;
  • low numbers of stomata/sunken stomata;
  • hairs to reduce turbulence. [any 3 points] [3]

[Total: 3]

5 (a) SAN/Sinoatrial node [1]

(b) (i) slows heart rate [1]
    (ii) speeds up the rate [1]
    (iii) speeds up the rate [1]

[Total: 4]

Chapter 6 Genes and cell division

1 (a) metaphase [1]

(b) 4 [2]

[Total: 3]

2 (a) adenine and thymine are similar proportions because adenine binds with thymine; cytosine and guanine are similar proportions because cytosine binds with guanine [2]

(b) They should be identical in number but the scientists were operating at the limits of instrumentation. [1]

(c) Organic bases form the codes for different amino acids. Different sequences of amino acids form the different proteins specific to a species. [2]

[Total: 5]

Chapter 7 Classification and biodiversity

1 A = Prokaryotae
   B = Fungi
   C = Protoctista
   D = Plantae
   E = Animalia   [5]

                                          [Total: 5]

2 (a)

	Mistle-thrush	Song-thrush
Kingdom	**Animalia**	**Animalia**
Phylum	Chordata	Chordata
Class	Aves	**Aves**
Order	Passeriformes	Passeriformes
Family	**Turdidae**	**Turdidae**
Genus	**Turdus**	**Turdus**
Species	**viscivorus**	**ericetorum**

                                                  [3]
   (b) disruptive selection   [1]
                                          [Total: 4]

3 (a) N = 20

$$d = \frac{20 \times 19}{(3 \times 2) + (6 \times 5) + (2 \times 1) + (1 \times 0) + (4 \times 3) + (3 \times 2) + (1 \times 0)}$$

$$= \frac{380}{56} = 6.79 \qquad [2]$$

   (b) Biodiversity was lower in pond near feeding station.
        Difference may not be significant.   [2]

                                          [Total: 4]

Chapter 8 Human health and disease

1 (a) droplet infection   [1]

   (b) (i) carriers   [1]
        (ii) we do not know that they carry the pathogen
              as they display no symptoms, so the people do
              not avoid contact and pass on the bacteria   [2]

                                          [Total: 4]

2 (a) (i) ability to secrete more antibodies   [1]
        (ii) the antibodies have specific receptor sites
              which bind with the antigens; they have
              a flexible protein which changes angle to fit
              the antigens; antibodies result in the
              destruction of the antigen in some way/
              neutralise toxin/cluster around antigens then
              cause precipitation/cause agglutination   [3]
        (iii) are produced when body first exposed to
               antigen; remain in body to react quickly
               when exposed to same antigen again   [2]

   (b) when the immune system attacks the person's own
        cells; pernicious anaemia/rheumatoid arthritis   [2]

   (c) the influenza virus often mutates so lymphocytes
        take longer to produce antibodies   [1]
                                          [Total: 9]

Index

Index